NEW ENGLAND

The Elm Tree Cottage, Newport, Rhode Island.

JAN -- 2019

FROMMER'S

BED AND BREAKFAST GUIDES

NEW ENGLAND

MAINE, NEW HAMPSHIRE, VERMONT,
MASSACHUSETTS, RHODE ISLAND, CONNECTICUT

By GLENN OAKLEY, GALE ZUCKER, NAOMI BLACK,
TERRY BERGER, and ROBERTA GARDNER

Photographs by Glenn Oakley, Gale Zucker, and George W. Gardner

DESIGNED AND PRODUCED BY
ROBERT R. REID AND TERRY BERGER

MACMILLAN • USA

Frontispiece photograph: *The Elm Tree Cottage,*
Newport, Rhode Island.

917.4
FROMMER

Published by Macmillan Travel
A Prentice Hall Macmillan Company
1633 Broadway
New York, NY 10019

MACMILLAN is a registered trademark of Macmillian, Inc.

Library of Congress Card No. 1085-9810
ISBN 0-02-860881-X

A Robert Reid Associates production
Typeset in Bodoni Book by Monotype Composition Company, Baltimore
Produced by Mandarin Offset, Hong Kong
Printed in Hong Kong

1 2 3 4 5 6 7 8 9 10

CONTENTS

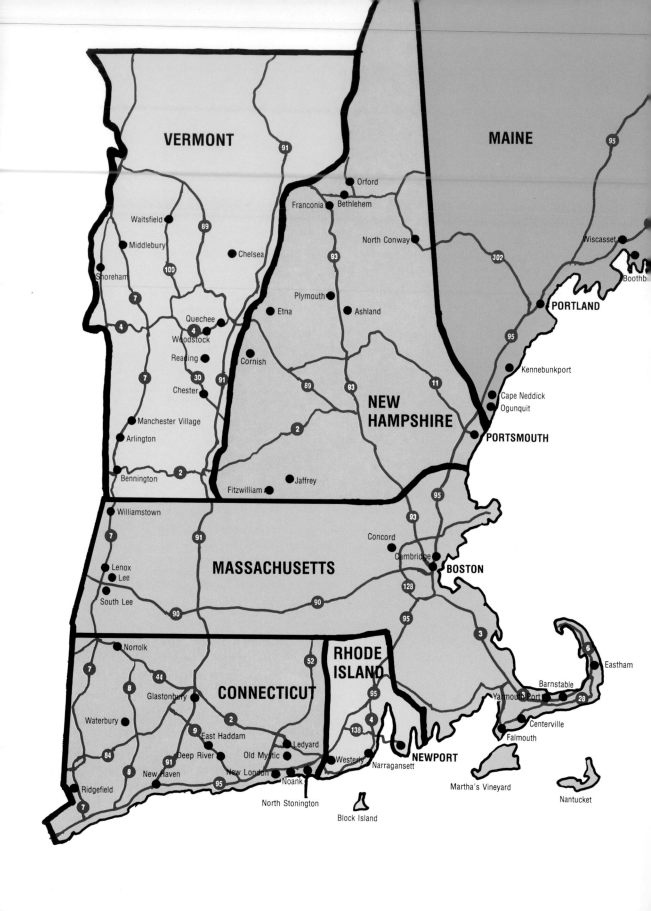

MAINE

Everything's shipshape

Captain Peter Smith calls his guests to breakfast with the familiar three-pitch call of a bosun's pipe. The affable Smith retired after thirty-six years in the U.S. Navy as a fighter pilot, but the Navy tradition lives on at The Maine Stay, which he runs with his wife, Donny, and her twin sister, Diana Robson.

The 1802 Federal-style house, painted white with black trim, is maintained in shipshape condition. "I like to keep things organized," notes Smith. He produces printed sheets on everything from recipes for the breakfast specialties to precise directions to the guests' next destination, with recommended stops along the way. He has filled a computer with these texts and distributes them upon request.

The house is set in Camden on Route 1, with extensive wooded and landscaped grounds behind and to the side. Paths wander through the grounds and continue up to Mt. Battie, from whose summit one can see all the way to Cadillac Mountain in Acadia National Park. Wooden decks around the house overlook the grounds.

Bedrooms range from large second-floor rooms appointed with family antiques to a ground-floor suite with glass doors opening out onto a private patio. This room features built-in bookshelves, window seats, and a glass-brick walled bathroom.

The massive house has a television room with a library of videos and books, two parlors with fireplaces, and a kitchen built around a nineteenth-century coal-burning cast iron stove, which is still used. Coffee beans are ground in a hand-cranked grinder each day.

Coffee and tea are set out at 6 A.M. and breakfast is served at 8:30 at a long dining table in a country-style room. The dining room floors are worth a second look: they're made of foot-wide planks milled about the time Thomas Jefferson was president.

MAINE STAY INN, 22 High St., Camden, ME 04843; (207) 236-9636; Peter Smith, Donny Smith, and Diana Robson, innkeepers and owners. Open all year. Eight rooms, six with private baths. Rates: $75 to $125, including breakfast. Children over 10 accepted; no pets; no smoking; Visa/MasterCard/American Express. Sailboat tours, whale-watching, sea-kayaking, hiking, antiques shopping, golf.

DIRECTIONS: two blocks north of Camden village center on Rte. 1.

Left below, breakfast is served family style.

A guest suite.

A white clapboard New England inn.

The entry hall.

The Jefferson Davis Room.

ABIGAIL'S

Personal and intimate

With just four guest rooms in this 1847 Greek Revival home, Abigail's maintains a personal and intimate atmosphere. Owners and innkeepers Donna and Ed Misner promote that atmosphere by serving everyone breakfast together at 8:30 A.M. at a single large table. They encourage their guests to meet and share stories. But for those preferring more privacy, breakfast can be brought to their bedroom on a tray set with china and flowers. Breakfast is plentiful, with a varying menu that includes soufflés, quiches, French toast, waffles, scones, muffins, and coffee cakes.

Abigail's is situated in the picturesque harbor village of Camden, on Route 1, just a few blocks from the town's center. The two-story home is bordered with a white wrought-iron fence, flowers and mature trees. The house was built by former Congressman E.K. Smart, whose friend, Jefferson Davis, was a frequent overnight guest.

The house has two common rooms on the main floor, both with fireplaces. One room is painted in a surprisingly pleasing combination of tangerine and green. Decanters of sherry are set out on silver trays, and Oriental carpets cover the wood floors.

Two guest rooms are located on the second floor and two suites are in the recently restored carriage

Left, Sherry is served by the fireside in the parlor.

house. The Copper Beech Suite is decorated in yellow, white, and blue and has a Jacuzzi. The Rose Garden Suite overlooks the garden. Both suites have mini-kitchens and televisions. Upstairs is the Jefferson Davis Room, with a canopied bed and overstuffed chairs by a reading table.

Wicker chairs on the covered front porch invite guests to settle down for a morning cup of coffee. A tree swing in the backyard hangs from the massive branch of a shade tree. A walk behind the house leads to the Mount Battie Trail, a short but invigorating hike that leads to a summit with grand views of Camden and the harbor.

ABIGAIL'S BED & BREAKFAST. 8 High St., Camden, ME 04843; (800) 292-2501; Donna and Ed Misner, owners. Open all year except March and April. Four rooms, all with private baths. Rates: $85 to $145, including breakfast. Children accepted; no pets; no smoking; Visa/MasterCard/American Express. Fine dining in Camden and area. Sailing, whale watching, hiking, skiing, golf.

DIRECTIONS: 2 blocks north of Camden Village.

A stunning brass bed in an airy guest room.

The original wood-paneled reception hall.

NORUMBEGA

An extraordinary stone mansion

Norumbega is an extraordinary stone mansion whose elusive exterior seems to change when viewed at different angles. Designed by A.B. Jennings of New York City, the Queen Anne style manse is quite unique. From one angle the house shows a wall of roughly faced cobblestones, punctuated by arched windows and a rounded, stepped roof. From another, it resembles a more common seaside cottage with a wide porch and bay windows. Looking at the entrance, the *porte cocherè*, and turret, the structure appears to be predominantly wood and brick. Close inspection reveals at least three different shingle patterns on the turret, the name "Norumbega" and "1886"

tiled and set in the right bay, and fossils embedded in the stone to the left of the entrance.

Inside, the wood draws first notice. Triangular-sawn oak with a marked sheen forms the entryway and three stairs to a landing with fireplace and elaborately carved corner seating. Spiral spindles below the banister add a suitably delicate touch.

The double parlors and curved study boast their share of beautiful wood. Carved grotesques, as compelling as Notre Dame's gargoyles, flank the fireplace; a central wood carpet establishes the floor theme.

The house, restored to its full elegance, is a stunning home complete with mountain and water views. Murray Keatinge, the owner, affords gracious service and warm hospitality.

NORUMBEGA. 61 High St., Camden, ME 04843; (207) 236-4646, Fax (207) 236-0284; Murray Keatinge, host. Open all year. Twelve guest rooms, all with private baths, five with working fireplaces. Rates: $135 to $450 (for Penthouse Floor); additional person, $35; includes generous, full breakfast. Children over 7 welcome; no pets; smoking permitted in guest rooms only; all credit cards. Hiking, skiing, tennis, golf, ocean beach and freshwater lake, windjammer cruises, Lighthouse Museum in Rockland.

DIRECTIONS: follow Rte. 1 north through Camden. The inn is on the right about one mile from town.

The Pub Room is warm and inviting.

BLACK FRIAR INN

A British-style pub

Tucked in a side street of Bar Harbor, Maine's most popular resort town, the Black Friar Inn is within easy walking distance of all the town's attractions, yet removed from the bustle of its busy streets.

The turn-of-the-century Victorian house is a complex of gables and dormers, all cheerily underscored with window boxes full of geraniums. The house was restored in 1980, using architectural pieces from area mansions and churches. Stained-glass windows cast rainbow colors into bedrooms. A British-style pub has been recreated on the ground floor, with its fireplace casting a warm, golden glow on the dark wood-paneled interior. It is a popular place on cool spring and fall days.

The inn's seven bedrooms range from a first-floor suite with a king-size bed, sitting room, sofa-bed, and fireplace to small but interesting garret rooms with queen-size beds, pedestal sinks, and private bathrooms.

Breakfast is served in the Sun Room on a long communal table. Fresh bread is baked daily, accompanying the main course, along with fruit, coffee, tea, and juices. The common room has a television, small library and refrigerator with soft drinks and mineral water.

Acadia National Park is only a short bicycle ride from the inn, and innkeepers Perry and Sharon Risley provide a map of the town and park.

BLACK FRIAR INN, 10 Summer St., Bar Harbor, ME 04609-1424; (207) 288-5091; Perry and Sharon Risley, owners. Seven rooms, all with private baths. Rates: $90 to $140, including breakfast. Children over 12 accepted; no pets; no smoking; Visa/MasterCard. Acadia National Park, Bar Harbor, whale-watching, sea-kayaking, sailboat cruises, plenty of fine restaurants.

DIRECTIONS: coming into Bar Harbor, turn left off Cottage St. across from Shop 'N Save.

CLEFTSTONE MANOR

Preserves the mood of Victorian gentility

James Blair built his summer home, a modest thirty-three room cottage, high on a rocky ledge overlooking the beautiful isle of Bar Harbor. His winter home in Washington, D.C., later used as an alternate presidential residence known as Blair House, sat across from the White House. Today both homes welcome travelers, Blair House serving as a home to dignitaries visiting the United States. Cleftstone Manor, under the new ownership of Pattie and Don Reynolds, is a stately bed and breakfast inn for guests visiting New England.

The entire house is furnished with fine antiques, including such unusual pieces as Joseph Pulitzer's awesome writing table. This grand table amply fills the formal dining room and is put to use each day when it is laden with home-baked goodies at tea time and with cheeses and wine in the evening. Breakfast is served in the formal dining room or on the enclosed sunporch, a light-washed room complemented by white wicker furniture, a collection of Delft china, and masses of greenery.

The bedrooms, each different, are decorated with a confident and sophisticated touch. A favorite for honeymooners is the spacious Romeo and Juliet Room. One corner is given over to a brass canopied bed, draped in white lace. A comfortable love seat faces a working fireplace and the beautifully detailed coffered ceiling deepens the prevailing sense of privacy and luxury. The Glastonbury Room, with high-back Victorian bedstead, red velvet chair, hand-crocheted bedspread, and many decorative grace notes is serene.

CLEFTSTONE MANOR, Eden St., Bar Harbor, ME 04609; (800) 962-9762, (207) 288-4951; Patty and Don Reynolds, owners. Open May 1 to Oct. 31. Fourteen double rooms, three suites, 5 with fireplaces, 4 with balconies; all with private baths. Rates: $95 to $198 per room, including full breakfast buffet, afternoon tea, and evening wine and cheese. Numerous restaurants nearby. Children over 8 welcome; no pets; Visa/MasterCard/Discover; no smoking.

DIRECTIONS: from points south, take Rte. 1 north to Ellsworth, then follow Rte. 3 into Bar Harbor. Inn is 500 feet past Bluenose Ferry terminal.

Joseph Pulitzer's writing table in the formal dining room.

Elegant four-poster beds in beautifully decorated guest rooms.

THE TIDES

Rooms with a view

The Tides, one of Bar Harbor's beautiful old summer cottages, is an 1887 white-columned Greek Revival with an acre of lawn stretching down to the ocean. Located on Frenchman's Bay in the historic part of town, the eighteen-room home is elegantly proportioned. There is a wrap-around porch with working fireplace that guests adore, and the white wicker furniture allows them to sit and enjoy the fire, the ocean, and the bountiful breakfast that is usually served there—perhaps cranberry-walnut pancakes,

herb-scrambled egg with dill sauce, or blueberry stuffed French toast.

Three light and airy rooms are available for guests, including the master suite with a working fireplace. All of the rooms are turned out in Laura Ashley finery, and all offer full ocean views.

The formal dining room has cherrywood furniture and a fireplace, and the most amazing twenty-one foot window seat and picture windows overlooking the Atlantic. The parlor, bathed in dusty blues and sand, is adorned with an 1868 Chickering piano, three overstuffed sofas, and of course, a water view.

Sunset schooner sailing, sea kayaking, and nature cruises are popular activities. The bed and breakfast is one block form the town pier and within walking distance of town, where there are fine restaurants and gift shops.

Majestically beautiful Acadia National Park, a legacy of the Rockefellers, occupies most of the island. It offers countless trails for hiking, horseback riding, bicycling, and cross-country skiing.

THE TIDES. 119 West Street, Bar Harbor, ME 04609; (207) 288-4968; Tom and Bonnie Sawyer, innkeepers. Open May 1 to Nov. 1. Three guest suites with private baths, queen-sized beds, and ocean views. Rates: $215 to $245 high season; $125 to $155 off season. Includes full breakfast. Inquire about children; no pets; no smoking; Visa/MasterCard.

DIRECTIONS: take Rte. 3 into Bar Harbor and turn left on West St. at first intersection (no light, but there is an island).

SQUIRE TARBOX

In a pastoral setting

The goats are usually a surprise, says innkeeper Bill Mitman. Guests come to the Squire Tarbox Inn for its pastoral, off-the-beaten-track solitude, its fabulous meals, and its blend of eighteenth and nineteenth-century architecture.

Still, the fact that Karen and Bill Mitman also operate a small, but high quality, goat dairy gives the Squire Tarbox a special ambience. The country farm flavor is not fabricated for the benefit of tourists; it's the genuine article.

And then there's the benefit of fresh, soft-herbed chèvre with crackers served on the screened deck or by the fire before dinner.

The inn is located on Westport Island, south of Wiscasset and adjacent to popular Boothbay Harbor. The major tourist attractions are readily accessible by car, but the relative seclusion of the inn is now one of its major attractions.

Left, the living room in the Carriage Barn.

The original wood-beamed house, now used as the dining room, was built in 1763. The original timbers and flooring remain. In 1825, Squire Samuel Tarbox added the more elegant and refined main house, which has also been well preserved. A carriage barn, which once separated the house from the livestock barn, has been converted to a cathedral-ceilinged parlor. Barn doors, which create one wall of the room, are opened in the summer, leaving an entire wall of windows. A cast-iron stove provides warmth on cool days.

Seven bedrooms with queen-sized beds have been created in the original barn, retaining rustic charm without sacrificing comforts. Four more guest rooms are in the 1825 section of the house. These bedrooms, like the new part of the house, are more refined.

Because of its secluded location, the inn offers exceptional gourmet dinners at 7 P.M. in the hand-hewn wood-beamed dining room. Cocktails are available from an open honor bar just off the front parlor.

THE SQUIRE TARBOX INN. RR 2, Box 620, Wiscasset, ME 04578; (207) 882-7693; Karen and Bill Mitman, owners. Open mid-May through October. Eleven rooms, all with private baths. Rates: $75 to $166, including breakfast; $102 to $220, including breakfast and dinner. Exquisite dinners served to guests and public. Mountain bikes and rowboat on premises; close to harbors, beaches, antiques shopping.

DIRECTIONS: take Rte. 144 south off Rte. 1 onto Westport Island and follow signs.

A 1786 colonial building.

KENNISTON HILL INN

Boothbay's most historic inn

Built in 1786, this center-chimney Colonial structure is Boothbay's most historic inn. With working fireplaces in both common rooms ablaze in winter weather and open windows capturing breezes in the summer, the inn is perfect all year round.

A pewter collection rests on the parlor's two-hundred-year-old cherry mantelpiece, flanked by wing back chairs and an Oriental rug. Tin wall sconces, baskets, a butter churn, and butter molds add interest to the décor. Well-polished fine reproduction furniture is placed throughout the inn.

Owner David Straight, a cabinet maker, has made his mark in the kitchen with savory three-cheese pie with tomatoes and sweet basil, ham and cheese in puff pastry, and peaches and cream French toast. Susan, his wife, adds to the mix with fresh-squeezed juices, fruit, coffee, and teas.

KENNISTON HILL INN. Rte. 27, Boothbay, ME 04537; (800) 992-2915, (207) 633-2159 (same for Fax); Susan and David Straight, owners. Open all year. White clapboard colonial built in 1786, on 4½ acres. Ten guest rooms, five with working fireplaces, all with private baths. Rates: $69 to $110, double; $25 for additional person. Full breakfast served. Children over ten preferred; no pets; no smoking; MasterCard/Visa. 9-hole golf course, boating, tennis, horseback riding, antiquing nearby. Varied dining at the harbor.

DIRECTIONS: from Rte. 1 turn onto Rte. 27 south to Boothbay. The inn is on a knoll on the left.

The breakfast room, like most of the house, is furnished simply in deference to the colonial tradition. Pale yellow pineapple paper picks up the soft specks of gold and brown in the braided rug and the tawny hues of the pine sideboard. What makes Kenniston Hill most appealing, though, are the five guest rooms with working fireplaces. A spotlessly maintained colonial restoration, Kenniston Hill is perfect for all-season beachcombers and high-season sailors.

Beamed ceilings and a 200-year-old cherry mantel.

FIVE GABLES INN

Quiet serenity

The Five Gables Inn is ideally situated for travelers who want to get away from other tourists. It is a haven of peace and quiet overlooking the water at the end of a winding country road, where the only sounds to be heard are the cries of seagulls wheeling overhead.

Local innkeepers Ellen and Paul Morissette recognized the potential of the unused inn. It had been a haven to the former owners when they arrived in the 1930s, as refugees from Nazi Germany.

Protected as a landmark, the inn was restored and rebuilt at the same time. Today, it offers all the latest amenities along with the flavor of painted wooden V-joint carpentry.

The walls of the rooms and hallways have been tastefully decorated by the Morissette's daughter-in-law, Nadine, with a variety of serigraphs, lithographs, old photographs, dried flowers, crazy quilts, and even framed needlepoint pictures.

One welcome addition to the original design is a large veranda that overlooks the water, as does the large public reception room, where a full breakfast is served buffet-style. Paul was a restaurateur for twenty years, and has developed a menu that varies from quiches and chili stratas to blueberry pancakes, French toast with maple syrup, and egg dishes with homemade biscuits—all served with fresh fruit.

FIVE GABLES INN. Murray Hill Rd., East Boothbay, ME 04544; (800) 451-5048, (207) 633-4551; Ellen and Paul Morissette, owners. Open mid-May to mid-Nov. Sixteen guest rooms with private baths; 5 with working fireplaces, all with views, except one. Rates: $90 to $140 per room, including full buffet breakfast. Children over 8 welcome; no pets; smoking on veranda only; Visa/MasterCard. Excellent seafood restaurants, including Maxfield's and The Lobsterman's Wharf in Boothbay Harbor.

DIRECTIONS: from Portland take I-95 north to exit 22 to Brunswick and US-1 east to Rte. 27 south towards Boothbay Harbor. At junction with Rte. 96 turn left on 96 and wind past shipyard to general store and junction with Murray Hill Rd., which should be followed to inn at end of road.

Even on a cloudy day, the view at breakfast time is exhiliarting.

THE POMEGRANATE INN

Artful Lodgings

The soft-grey façade of this Victorian reveals nothing of its interior. But, open the door and surprises burst forth as they do from a Fabergé Easter egg. A real treat is in store for you!

Isabel and Alan Smiles, collectors of museum-quality art, and decorators *extraordinaire*, have produced a house that is difficult to leave. Heidi Gerquest's hand-painted designs on bedroom walls—from fantasy birds to roses in bloom—would inspire Matisse. American, English, and Chinese antiques blend harmoniously with Oriental floor coverings and hand-painted floors. Hand-lacquered halls feature modern-crafted pieces that enliven the space. Bathrooms with Grecian-marbled floors and faux-marbled touches on cornices and tubs are not to be missed.

Left, two of the superb guest rooms, showing the decorative walls that were painted by hand.

Our color coordinated author, Terry Berger, blends perfectly with the handpainted walls of a Pomegranate guest room.

You keep wishing you could sleep in *all* the guest rooms. A Johnny Ross painting, Jamie Burt's perfect egg, and Tommy Simpson's whimsical cupboard vie for attention. And covering the walls are the vibrant watercolors and sensual floral oil paintings by artist Winifred Mury, the Smiles' relative who painted for over 60 years, and predicted that she would be famous only after she died.

A hot breakfast prepared by the host is served on a hand-painted table, and is so artfully presented that it becomes a part of the surrounding art collection.

Staying here offers you the pleasure of meeting wonderful people who appreciate and collect beautiful things, and are willing to share their treasures with their guests.

THE POMEGRANATE INN. 49 Neal Street, Portland, ME 04102; (207) 772-1006; (800) 356-0408; Fax (207) 773-4426; Alan and Isabel Smiles, owners. Open all year. Eight guest rooms with private baths. Rates: $125 to $155; $95 to $125 per room off season, including full breakfast. Children over 16 welcome; no pets; no smoking; all major credit cards. Portland's charmingly restored historic district is alive with restaurants and shops. Activities include boat rides and whale-watching.

DIRECTIONS: call for directions, which vary depending on where you are.

An unforgettable place to have breakfast.

BUFFLEHEAD COVE

A hideaway on the Kennebunk River

Perched on the banks of the Kennebunk River as it flows out to sea, Bufflehead Cove offers a secluded getaway on the edge of one of southern Maine's most popular resorts.

The Victorian "cottage" sits on six acres of landscaped grounds—rolling lawns, sea-wind-sculpted pines, and flower gardens. The large gray clapboard house faces out onto the river. From the covered deck, guests can look downstream to the bustle of downtown Kennebunkport, a village of churches, fine restaurants, art galleries and artisan shops. But here, just a short distance away, herons stalk the shallows, and the distinctive sea ducks for which the inn is named return each autumn.

Bufflehead Cove offers six bedrooms, each with a private bath. The Hideaway is a spacious room with a

Left above, the inn is nestled in the trees by the riverside. Below, the spacious Hideaway Room.

painted tile fireplace in the center. A wall of windows looks out over the river and private deck. The bath includes a Jacuzzi. The upstairs River Room features a folk art collection and balcony overlooking the river. The Garden Studio has a private entrance and patio and is lavishly decorated with flower bouquets.

Breakfast is served at 8:30 A.M. on the deck or in the wood-paneled dining room. A typical breakfast includes fresh-squeezed orange juice, ginger-poached pears in an English custard sauce, apple-stuffed French toast, and maple-glazed sausage, with abundant coffee and tea. A spacious and airy living room with a fireplace and Persian rugs looks out over the river.

Bufflehead Cove is innkeeper Harriet Gott's family home. Her husband, James, is a commercial fisherman. The bed and breakfast is reached by a gravel lane that winds through the seaside forest.

BUFFLEHEAD COVE. Box 499, Kennebunkport, ME 04046; (207) 967-3879; James and Harriet Gott, owners. Open all year. Six rooms, all with private baths. Rates: $85 to $190, including breakfast. No children; no pets; no smoking; Visa/MasterCard/Discover. Gourmet dining and lobster pounds in town. Whale-watching, swimming beaches, lobster boat rides, golf, boat rides.

DIRECTIONS: take Rte. 95 to exit 3, turn left on 35 south. At intersection of Rte. 1 and 35, continue on 35 for 3.1 miles. Turn left on gravel lane and follow to inn.

Breakfast room in the main house.

OLD FORT INN

Kennebunkport charm

The Old Fort Inn is a charming carriage house-lodge combination that invites travelers for long-term stays. The sixteen color-coordinated American and English country-style rooms come with cable color television, some with efficiency kitchens stocked with ironstone plates, wine glasses, pans, tea kettle, toaster, napkins and placemats—even laundry facilities.

It's one-and-a-fifth miles from the inn to town, an easy bike ride past lovely frame cottages and old sea captains' houses. Kennebunkport retains much of its late nineteenth-century atmosphere when ship building gave way to the tourist industry. Wealthy summer visitors built wisely and well, keeping the village quaint and relatively small. The inn's location, just one block from the rocky shore, is also adjacent to Cape Arundel, where some of the most handsome turn-of-the-century cottages still stand.

Kennebunkport offers a rich variety of activities: trolley rides, scenic cruises, sailing lessons, yacht charters, and whale watching are but a few. The sports menu complements what the Old Fort Inn has to offer on its grounds. A swimming pool, shuffleboard area, and tennis court bridge the gap between the guest rooms and the main lodge where breakfast is served.

Sheila and David Aldrich and their daughter oversee the homemade muffins, fresh-baked breads, and fresh fruit for the buffet breakfast. Friendships often begin at the morning meal and extend into the evening hours around the pool.

The Old Fort Inn presents the best of what casual adult resorts can provide: a relaxed atmosphere amid pleasant surroundings.

OLD FORT INN. Old Fort Ave., Kennebunkport, ME 04046; (800) 828-3678, (207) 967-5353, Fax (207) 967-9761; Sheila and David Aldrich, hosts. Open mid-April to mid-December. Fourteen guest rooms plus two suites, all with private baths and wet bars; some with Jacuzzis. Rates: $125 to $175; suites $230 to $260; additional person, $20. Rates include buffet breakfast and one hour of tennis daily. Children over 12 welcome; no pets; no smoking; American Express/MasterCard/Visa/Discover. Pool on premises.

DIRECTIONS: take exit 3 from I-95 and turn left on Rte. 35 for 5½ miles. Turn left at light at Sunoco station and go .3 miles to Colony Hotel and turn left and follow signs to inn.

Each guest room has a kitchenette.

INN AT HARBOR HEAD

Right on Maine's lobster coast

Artistry, elegance, and natural beauty in equal measure are the prime qualities of life at the Inn at Harbor Head. This intimate bed and breakfast is located on Kennebunkport's Cape Porpoise Bay, an idyllic lobstering cove whose sparkling waters are dotted with bobbing boats, rocky islands, and lighthouses that twinkle in the distance. Joan and Dave Sutter own the inn, a turn-of-the-century, weathered-shingle home that rambles along a promontory overlooking a sheltered harbor and the bay beyond.

Inside, the Sutters have created an elegant world that is sophisticated enough for the pages of a stylish home magazine. The inn's common rooms are furnished in a refined style, the living room displaying a crystal chandelier, a handsome Japanese screen, fine oriental rugs, and softly-lit oil paintings of the Sutters' ancestors. But real artistry is revealed in the five guest bedrooms. Joan is a seasoned artist—or, in her words, "a former three-dimensional artist now changed to 'wall painter' "—whose genius for color and de-

sign is wedded to an equally accomplished technical skill. Each bedroom plays out a romantic theme embellished by Joan's lyrical, painted imaginings inspired by the bay and surrounding village.

THE INN AT HARBOR HEAD. Pier Road, Cape Porpoise, RR 2, Box 1180, Kennebunkport, ME 04046; (207) 967-5564; Dave and Joan Sutter, hosts. Open all year, except Dec. 20 to March 31. Five rooms with private baths, some with fireplaces and balconies. Rates: $140 to $240, with full gourmet breakfast. Children over 12 welcome; no pets; Visa/MasterCard; smoke-free environment. Swimming from inn's dock. Whale watching, art galleries, summer theater, antiquing in area. Dining nearby.

DIRECTIONS: from Maine Turnpike take exit 3 and follow Rte. 9 east through Kennebunkport Village to Cape Porpoise. Leave Rte. 9 at hardware store and take the road to the pier for ³⁄₁₀ miles to inn on right.

The Harbor Suite has hand-painted murals in both rooms.

CAPTAIN LORD MANSION

A classic

The Captain Lord Mansion is one of the classic American bed & breakfast inns. Bev Davis and Rick Litchfield have run this imposing inn since 1978, and they've learned how to do it right.

The mansion was built during the War of 1812 by Nathaniel Lord, who built and operated a fleet of merchant ships. The mansion passed down through the Lord family for several generations. The family's lineage is recorded in the front hallway, and family portraits hang throughout the massive house. Antiques, from rocking horses to cabinets, decorate the inn.

The three-story yellow clapboard mansion sits on a hill above Kennebunkport. Brick walkways lead from the parking area through the landscaped lawn to the main entrance. The inn has sixteen guest rooms located on three floors. The rooms, named after ships built by Captain Lord and his kin, are spacious and decorated with fine antiques and linens. Ship Harvest

Left above, the Ship Harvest Room. Below, the Ship Merchant Room.

on the third floor has a king-size four-poster bed opposite a gas fireplace. A sofa and chair are set in the center of the room and an antique desk is set off to the side. An entryway serves as a large closet and has a refrigerator stocked with juices, soft drinks, and mineral water.

A nearby stairway leads to the cupola atop the mansion, its circular glass walls providing a 360-degree view. Downstairs on the main floor is a gift shop and the main parlor, a large room that, like the rest of the house, is decorated in beautiful antique furniture and carpets. Coffee, tea, and the day's newspapers are set out in the parlor each morning. Breakfast is served in shifts at 8:30 and 9:30 A.M. in the dining room around the corner. Dining is family style in a kitchen fronted with a cast-iron stove and two long dining tables.

The inn has a separate game room and provides beach towels and beach parking passes for guests.

THE CAPTAIN LORD MANSION. Box 800, Kennebunkport, ME 04046; (207) 967-3141; Bev Davis and Rick Litchfield, owners. Open all year. Sixteen rooms, all with private baths. Rates: $149 to $249, including breakfast. Children six and older accepted; no pets; no smoking; Visa/MasterCard. Abundant dining in town, ranging from very casual to five-star. Galleries, shops, beaches, fishing, whale-watching, scenic cruises.

DIRECTIONS: from I-95 take exit 3 left onto Rte. 35 for 5½ miles to Rte. 9 east. Turn left, go over bridge and take first right onto Ocean Avenue. Take fifth left off Ocean Ave.

A spacious third-floor guest room

THE CAPTIAN JEFFERDS INN

A New England sea captain's house

The Kennebunkport historic district is peppered with gracious "cottages" built in the early 1800s by seafaring captains who traveled the globe in their sailing ships and returned with untold treasures with which they furnished their homes.

Warren Fitzsimmons had a successful antiques business when he bought one of these—Captain Jefferds' home—and brought the place to vibrant life. If, upon entering, you have a sense of *déjà vu*, don't doubt your feelings. The work of this gifted innkeeper has been featured on the covers of several prestigious home decorating magazines.

Two cobalt blue vases displaying a bounty of brilliant silk flowers flank the formal entryway. To the left is the breakfast room, where guests gather each morning to be served excellent fare. Warren mans the kitchen, preparing custardy French toast, delicate pancakes, and perfectly turned eggs.

Eash guest room is special. Several are decorated in Laura Ashley's simple prints; others are dressed in muted tones that dramatize an elegant chaise, bird's-eye maple chest, or Chinese screen.

The collection of antiques in this inn is endlessly fascinating. Warren buys only the truest examples to represent a period—there are no reproductions in the entire inn—and the place practically vibrates from the beauty produced by his stunning collection. Though Warren was personally attracted to American antiques, from tramp and shell art to twig furniture and Indian baskets, the inn's formal lines required sterling silver and crystal as well. It all works.

THE CAPTAIN JEFFERDS INN. Pearl St., P.O. Box 691, Kennebunkport, ME 04046; (207) 967-2311; Warren Fitzsimmons, host. 1804 Federal style sea captain's house. Open all year except closed during January, February, March. Twelve guest rooms in main house, all private baths; 4 suites, 2 with kitchenettes in attached 18th-century carriage house. Rates $85 single, $85 to $145 double; suites $155–165 per day, in season; guests are treated to full breakfast, with seasonal specialties. Children welcome; pets welcome with advance notice; smoking not permitted; Visa/MasterCard.

DIRECTIONS: take Maine Turnpike to exit 3 to Rte. 35. Follow signs through Kennebunk to Kennebunkport. Turn left at traffic light and cross drawbridge. Turn right at monument onto Ocean Ave. Proceed ³⁄₁₀ miles to Arundel Wharf and turn left onto Pearl Street.

A stunning restoration

Right off Route 1, sometimes called the "antique row of New England," the Wooden Goose Inn corners off its own country garden in full view of the Cape Neddick River. Guests gazing out from the glassed-in breakfast room overlook the perennial blooms and a specially commissioned Chippendale garden bench. The bench is just one of interior designer Jerry Rippetoe's unique additions to this intimate country house. Partner Tony Sienicki, the other half of this able team, attends to most of the carpentry and finishing.

The precision restoration began June 15, 1983, the day they bought the house. By July 2, after working twenty-two-hour days, Jerry and Tony welcomed their first overnight visitors. The quick revitalization succeeded only because of professional foresight and months of planning and preparation. "The day we looked at it we took measurements," remarked Tony.

The result is stunning. A true overabundance of Victorian paraphernalia blends with revitalized Orientalia. The focus in the reception room rests

on the hand-carved, hand-painted cormondel screen, a black lacquer on teak *chef-d'oeuvre* that hints at other treasures inside. Guests are rarely disappointed with the many beautiful touches.

Excess and elegance are synonymous here. Twenty-eight yards of chintz drape down from one canopy. The clawfoot tub of bedroom number 4 stands in regal spaciousness next to a bentwood rocker, a combination that inspires guests to bring their own bubble bath and champagne.

Morning starts with elaborate breakfasts served on Lenox china with silver and linen asides. Plans to replace Sheelan crystal with Waterford illustrate the dynamics of the Wooden Goose. Every January the doors close for redecoration. Balloon shades change to miniblinds; greens give way to blues. The transformation keeps the inn vital—and keeps guests returning year after year.

THE WOODEN GOOSE INN. Rte. 1, Cape Neddick, ME 03902; (207) 363-5673; Tony Sienicki and Jerry Rippetoe, hosts. Open August through June. Six guest rooms, all with private baths. Rates: $125, including an elegant, hearty breakfast which changes every day. Afternoon tea. Dining nearby. Children over 12 welcome; no pets; no credit cards. The ocean is one mile from the inn. Golf, tennis, bicycling in Ogunquit. Fine dining at Cape Neddick Inn and Portobello in Portsmouth.

DIRECTIONS: take I-95 to the York exit (No. 1, marked "last exit before toll"). Turn north on Rte. 1 for 3.4 miles. The inn is on the right, five houses after the junction of Rtes. 1 and 1A.

The sunny lounge and breakfast room.

HARTWELL HOUSE

Lifestyles of the rich and famous

The Hartwell House is as close to perfect as life allows. When things seem out of control, this is a special oasis that offers solace, serenity, and service. Every need is anticipated by innkeepers Trisha and Jim Hartwell to insure that all is flawless for the duration of your stay.

Furnished with period pieces of simple elegance in the main house, and a more contemporary and lighter feeling in the House on the Hill across the way, the feeling is similar in both—a successful blending of the outdoors with the interior space, in colors so pure and furnishings so simple that it has a calming effect on guests.

Balconies with picture-perfect flower boxes look over Perkins Cove, once a famous artists' colony, and now a bustling sea village of lobster shacks, restaurants, boutiques, and shops. All of this is just a mile from the sand dunes and the beautiful three-mile beach.

The Abenaki Indians' word Ogunquit means "Beautiful Place by the Sea." The same can be said about the Hartwell House.

HARTWELL HOUSE. 118 Shore Road, Ogunquit, ME 03907; (207) 646-7210; Jim and Trisha Hartwell, Anne and Bill Mozingo, innkeepers. Open all year. Sixteen rooms, suites, and apartments in 2 houses, all with private baths, air conditioning, and parking. Rates: $100 to $175 double, including full gourmet breakfast (off-season rates after Nov. 1). Inquire about children; no pets; no smoking; Visa/MasterCard/American Express. Extravagant seafood dining within walking distance at famous Perkins Cove. Beaches and dunes for fresh air and swimming. Golf privileges at Cape Neddick Country Club.

DIRECTIONS: from Portland take scenic Rte. 1 through Ogunquit/Shore Road to inn.

The décor is elegantly restrained.

NEW HAMPSHIRE

SISE INN

Restored to its former glory

Home to one of the area's leading maritime merchants when Portsmouth was "the fishing and ship-building capital of the New World," the Sise Inn has been restored to its former glory.

Owned by a group that restores historic properties as bed and breakfasts in the United States and Canada, the Sise Inn provides comforts and amenities that suit the business traveler and tourist alike. Twenty-five rooms and nine suites individually decorated in period pieces, easily accommodate families and groups. Original carved woodwork, moldings, and decorative fireplaces supply interest and warmth.

Served in the breakfast room every morning, a buffet includes muffins, bagels, yogurt, cheese, and cereals. Breakfast may also be enjoyed on the adjoining sun porch.

Restaurants in the area that merit mention are The Dolphin Striker, as well as The Library Restaurant, which is located in the old Rockingham mansion which dates back to 1785. The Library Restaurant features American cuisine, and shelves filled with yards of vintage books.

Sise Inn manager Carl Jensen is eager to please, and is the recipient of the New Hampshire Innkeeping Award for 1989. Guests will most certainly find an award-winning bed and breakfast here.

SISE INN. 40 Court Street, Portsmouth, NH 03801; (800) 267-0525; (603) 433-1200 (same for Fax); Carl Jensen, manager. Open all year. 34 guest rooms, all with private baths. Rates: $89 to $175 double, including continental breakfast buffet. Children over 6 welcome; no pets; smoking allowed; Danish spoken; Visa/MasterCard/American Express/Diners Club. Inn has 3 conference and reception rooms with audio-visual equipment.

DIRECTIONS: right off I-95 in downtown Portsmouth; ask for detailed directions.

The elegant dining room.

The Captain's Room.

GOVERNOR'S HOUSE

The innkeeper's artistry abounds

A stately Georgian colonial house built in 1917, the Governor's House served as the family home of former New Hampshire Governor Charles Dale for 30 years. Proprietors Nancy and John Grossman bought the home in 1991 and converted it into an elegant and friendly bed and breakfast.

The house is situated on a quiet residential street within easy walking distance of historic Portsmouth. There are four guest rooms, each individually decorated. Beautiful handmade quilts adorn the queen-size beds. Guests may be inspired to linger in the showers here; Nancy Grossman is a professional tile painter and artist and she has created scenes of whimsy and wonder in all the home's baths.

The Peacock Room, decorated in art nouveau style, has a tile mural of The Lady and The Peacock

Left below, the entrance hall and stairway.

on the walls of the shower for two. A mermaid floats on the walls of the shower in the Captain's Room.

The house has a parlor with a fireplace and wall mural. On the second floor French doors open into an intimate TV and lounging room. Coffee and tea are set out early each morning. The former dining room on the ground floor is banked with windows and has its own fireplace for cool mornings. A bottomless cookie jar is maintained in this room. And guests can choose to play tennis on the private court next to the house—or play the baby grand piano.

There is plenty to do and see in this thriving port town. The best known attraction, just a few blocks from the Governor's House, is the Strawbery Banke Museum, where a collection of colonial houses and buildings from the 1600s to the 1900s has been preserved. The ten-acre living museum documents the evolution of the area over four centuries.

GOVERNOR'S HOUSE BED & BREAKFAST. 32 Miller Ave., Portsmouth, NH 03801; (603) 431-6546; John and Nancy Grossman, owners. Open all year. Four rooms, all with private baths. Rates: $65 to $140, including breakfast. Children over 14 accepted; no pets; no smoking indoors; Visa/MasterCard/American Express. Over 30 good restaurants within walking distance. Strawbery Banke Museum, harbor tours, whale-watching, beaches, golf nearby. Tennis on premises.

DIRECTIONS: from I-95 take exit 5 to the Portsmouth Traffic Circle. Go half-way around circle and take North Bypass 1 to Maplewood exit. Turn right at stop sign and go 8/10 mile to stop light at Rte. 1 and Jct. 1A, then left on Miller for one block.

A mermaid adorns the tiles of the shower in the Captain's Room.

A mural by innkeeper Nancy Grossman decorates the parlor.

People love it here.

MOOSE MOUNTAIN LODGE

Casual, with lots of fireplaces

Moose Mountain Lodge virtually spills over the western slope of Moose Mountain. Porch-sitters recline in full view of unspoiled countryside, where Vermont's Green Mountains rise out of the clear, smooth-running waters of the Connecticut River.

Just seven miles northeast of Hanover, home of Dartmouth College, the lodge is a back-country hideaway on 350 acres, situated on a dirt cul de sac that ends at the top of a ridge. Between the lodge and the mountaintop the road is veined with numerous trails, far away from the whoosh of passing traffic and noisy crowds. Winter skiers and summer hikers can disappear into the woods and feel secluded.

Inside, Kay and Peter Shumway cater to nature-lovers who gather around one of three common-room fireplaces. The stone fireplace in the living room warms-up conversation as much as it does noses and toes.

"You can put your feet up here," says Kay, who emphasizes that her guests feel relaxed in the fresh, clean, and comfortable lodge.

After dinner many folks head down to the bar room (BYOB) to play ping-pong, darts, or a board game by yet another native stone fireplace, this one mottled with garnet-studded rose quartz. A working player piano livens up the evening with classic old favorites. Once the music's over, guests retire to appropriately rustic bedrooms made especially homey with handmade spruce log or other wooden beds and muted linens.

MOOSE MOUNTAIN LODGE. Etna, NH 03750; (603) 643-3529; Kay and Peter Shumway, innkeepers. Open January to mid-March and June to late October. Twelve cozy rooms share five modern bathrooms. Rates: $60 per person, including hearty full breakfast. American plans available. Children welcome; no pets; no smoking. 50 km of cross-country ski trails; downhill skiing within 10 miles; hiking trails. Dartmouth College offers cultural events year-round.

DIRECTIONS: from exit 18 on Rte. 89, go north on Rte. 120 toward Hanover, ½ mile. Higbea Motel and Barbelle's Restaurant are on the left. Turn right here onto Etna Rd. into Etna Village. Go ½ mile past the Etna Store (phone from here if it's your first time) and turn right onto Rudsboro Rd. (just before the church). Go up Rudsboro Rd. 2 miles, then turn left on Old Dana Rd. and continue for ½ mile and turn right. Drive up the mountain one mile to the Lodge.

Decorative patterns in a guest room.

ADAIR

A Teapot Dome connection

On grounds landscaped by Frederick Olmstead, in a three-story house built by a Teapot Dome attorney, the Banfield family has created an elegant country inn with impeccable class and style.

Guests drive up the gently curved driveway bordered with rock walls and lined with mature trees to the white Georgian-style mansion. In the lobby, a printed card records the day's guests and their hometowns. Eight guest rooms are located on the second and third floors. These generous-sized rooms are lavishly decorated with period antiques and reproductions. All rooms have views of the White Mountains or the grounds. On the upper floors is a quiet alcove with an armchair, reading lamp, and bookshelves. A collection of turn-of-the-century hats lines the stairway.

On the main floor, a living room runs the length of the house, with sofas and chairs circling the fire-

Left above, gardens landscaped by Frederick Olmstead, who also did Central Park. Below, the parlor/sitting room.

The Granite Tap Room has a pool table.

place at one end and a chess table and reading chairs at the other. Opposite the entryway is the dining room where a full breakfast is served between 8 and 9 A.M. Standard fare includes fresh fruit, homemade oatmeal or granola, hot popovers, eggs Benedict, or quiche, alternated with blueberry pancakes or Murphy's Irish toast and Vermont cob-smoked bacon. Exquisite dinners are served on-site by the Tim-Bir Alley restaurant.

Downstairs, the walls of the Granite Tap Room are lined with black-and-white photos of the home's builder, attorney Frank Hogan, whose clients included Teddy Roosevelt, Andrew Mellon, and Edward Doheny. Hogan successfully defended Doheny against charges that he bribed Secretary of the Interior Albert Fall for oil-drilling rights on federal land at Teapot Dome, Wyoming. The grateful Doheny is said to have given Hogan a one million dollar bonus—in the same black bag with which he earlier bribed Fall.

ADAIR. Old Littleton Rd., Bethlehem, NH 03574; (800) 441-2606; Nancy, Pat and Hardy Banfield, owners. Eight rooms, all with private baths. Rates: $125 to $175, including breakfast and afternoon tea. No smoking; no pets; Visa/MasterCard/American Express. Tennis court on grounds; golf, skiing, hiking, Franconia and Crawford Notches, White Mountains National Forest nearby.
DIRECTIONS: turn off Hwy 93 at Bethlehem exit 40 and turn at Adair sign immediately after leaving highway.

Another guest room with different patterns.

Each guest room has its own personality.

VICTORIAN HARVEST

Lots of lace and antiques

This 1850s Victorian home sits on a quiet side street just off the busy thoroughfare that runs through the village of North Conway. It is conveniently close to the town's multitude of outlet stores and restaurants, yet removed from the hubub.

The yellow clapboard house is decorated in English country style, with lots of lace, floral fabrics and antiques. The inn offers six guest rooms, each with its own personality and its own teddy bear. Victoria Station is a large room with a bay window, brass bed and antique carousel horse. Cotswold Hideaway has a view of Mt. Washington, and Hidden Door features a headboard made from a wooden door. Two queen rooms, Heather Moor and Covent Gardens, are frequently combined as a suite for families or small groups.

Two common rooms downstairs are available for lounging. One room has a fireplace opposite the kitchen and dining room; the other is more private and features a library and a television/VCR with a selection of movies from which to choose.

A full country breakfast is served in a small, sunny dining area. Innkeepers Linda and Robert Dahlberg cook up something new each morning: Belgian waffles, quiches, coffee cakes and fruit plates, along with a variety of fresh juices and coffee.

Outside, a white picket fence borders the inn's swimming pool. Landscaped grounds surround the house.

VICTORIAN HARVEST INN. 28 Locust Lane, North Conway, NH 03860-1763; (800) 642-0749; Linda and Robert Dahlberg, owners. Open all year. Six rooms, two of which share a bathroom. Rates: $65 to $90 (subtract $10 for singles, add $15 for fall foliage season), including breakfast. Children over 5 accepted; no pets; no smoking; Visa/MasterCard/American Express/Discover. Hiking, skiing, White Mountains, shopping, swimming pool on premises.

DIRECTIONS: in North Conway; one mile north of Mountain Valley Mall, turn off Rte. 16 onto Locust Lane. Inn is at top of hill on left.

Swimming pool set in landscaped grounds.

The Cinnamon Room.

BUNGAY JAR

Much more than a restored barn

This bed and breakfast set in the middle of New Hampshire's White Mountains is as unique as its name, which refers to a jarring spring wind that rips through this part of the country.

The inn itself is a little harder to describe. The structure is an eighteenth-century barn that was disassembled, then moved and rebuilt to create a six-bedroom inn. The massive exposed beams that rise above the living room show the adze marks of the barn's original builder.

The Rose Suite has a private balcony that overlooks the open living room with its stone fireplace and antique artifacts. One of the most popular rooms—the Stargazer Suite—occupies the third floor. The stairway leading up to it has a railing made from antique lightning rods with glass balls. There are four skylights and the ceiling is decorated with stars and moons. A telescope stands opposite the king-sized bed, and there is a claw-foot tub in which to soak. The Hobbit Room has the feel of a tree house, with its French doors opening onto a private balcony amid tall pine trees. All guests have access to a small indoor sauna.

Balconies and decks wrap around the building at all levels, overlooking the extensive gardens created by innkeepers Kate Kerivan and Lee Strimbeck. The

Left above, the inn was originally an 18th-century barn. Below, the Stargazer Room.

gardens roll down from the house in a profusion of blossoms to a lily pond. Walking paths snake through the perennials and annuals, leading to the pond or taking off through the woods to a brook. The pond is home to colorful Japanese carp known as koi and is afloat with water lilies reminiscent of a Monet painting. A greenhouse next to the pond is also home to the innkeepers' pet iguana.

Sun tea and lemonade are served on the balconies each afternoon in the summer months. In winter, it is mulled cider and snacks by the fire. Full buffet-style breakfasts feature local smoked meats, baked goods and edible flowers from the garden.

THE BUNGAY JAR. Box 15, Easton Valley Rd., Franconia, NH 03580; (603) 823-7775; Kate Kerivan and Lee Strimbeck, owners. Open all year. Six rooms, four with private baths. Rates: $65 to $105, $75 to $130 mid-Sept. through Oct., including breakfast. School-age children accepted; no pets; no smoking indoors; Visa/MasterCard/American Express/Discover. White Mountains National Forest, Franconia Notch State Park, skiing, summer theater, antique shopping.

DIRECTIONS: from I-93 take exit 38 to Rte. 116 south for 5½ miles and look for carved wooden sign on left, 200 yards beyond Sugar Hill Rd.

The inn reflected in the colorful lily pond.

WHITE GOOSE INN

Cozy American with European panache

Orford is seated by the banks of the upper Connecticut River just across a bridge from Fairlee, Vermont. Originally a "fort town" built by the British, it soon hummed with activity from logging and agriculture. Seven "ridge houses" dating from between 1773 and 1839 form a stately white row by the green in the town's center.

The White Goose Inn is also celebrated for its elm tree growing through the circular colonial revival porch. Manfred and Karin Wolf adopted this brick and woodframe home and transformed it into a cozy American country classic with European panache.

Karin, a craftsperson whose work is evident throughout the inn, did all the delicate stenciling, made the pierced parchment lampshades, and cunningly assembled traveler's sewing kits for each impeccably designed, spotless guest room.

White geese are the house motif. A porcelain goose with a pink satin ribbon around its neck sits in the window; a cloth goose pokes its head out of a basket on the hutch; and an early American metal cut-out depicts a young girl followed by two geese. And there's a white wooden goose on the marble-topped treadle sewing machine base in the hall to greet guests when they arrive.

Breakfasts are very special here, reflecting the hosts' European heritage. Hearty home-baked goods look even more tempting on the Wolf's fine china.

The tasteful choices in furnishing and accessories are consistent throughout the White Goose. The parlor exudes the glow from an unusual porcelain chandelier. The dining room benefits from a beautifully crafted modern wood table and tall Shaker-style chairs.

This wonderful hideaway engages its guests, tempting them again and again to relax and sit back in an attractive setting where the details in every room please the eye.

THE WHITE GOOSE INN. Rte. 10, P.O. Box 17, Orford, NH 03777; (800) 358-4267, (603) 353-4812, Fax (603) 353-4543; Manfred and Karin Wolf. German spoken. Open all year. Fourteen guest rooms, most with private baths. Rates: $75 to $160, including a full country breakfast. No children under 8; no pets, with exceptions; no smoking. MasterCard/Visa. Hiking, biking trails, golf, skiing, sleigh rides; Saint-Gaudens National Historic Site. Dartmouth College, 15 miles.

DIRECTIONS: from I-91, take exit 15 (Fairlee, VT); cross the bridge to New Hampshire and take Rte. 10 south one mile. The inn is on the left. From I-93, take exit for I-89 and continue to Rte. 10 north. The inn is approximately 15 miles north of Hanover on the right.

Collecting maple syrup from the inn's own trees.

A perfect room.

THE GLYNN HOUSE

Where Victoriana abounds

Back in 1895 the biggest man in town was L. W. Packard, owner of the woolen mill, and Ashland's largest employer. The new house Mr. Packard built for his family that year was everything one would expect of a man of his position.

It was Queen Anne in style, with a cupola tower and wide, gingerbread porches. The inside was finished all in carved oak and decorated with wallpapers of the period. It was indeed a fine family mansion.

Now it is home to another family—the Patermans—and their many bed and breakfast guests.

Karol Paterman is a former restaurateur from Philadelphia, but is originally from Gdansk, the home of his fellow countryman President Lech Walesa, who worked at the famous Polish shipyard there. Betsy is also a restaurateur, and a native of Philadelphia, where she met Karol.

Together with Karol's mother as housekeeper *par excellence*, they chose the rewarding life of bed and breakfast hosts a couple of years ago, when they found the Packard mansion in central New Hampshire.

As avid collectors and auction goers, furnishing the house was right up their alley. Victorian antiques abound throughout the common rooms and the four guest rooms. One guest room in the tower is oval in shape, and offers an interesting furniture arrangement which includes a canopied bed and a Jacuzzi right in the room. There is a fireplace in another guest room, with a fine mahogany bed and interesting Victorian memorabilia, a plethora of which is displayed in the other rooms as well.

A delicious, full breakfast is served, varying from day-to-day, but fresh farmers' eggs are always a staple of the dishes prepared by the exhuberant hosts.

THE GLYNN HOUSE INN. 43 Highland St., Ashland, NH 03217; (603) 968-3775; Betsy and Karol Paterman, owners. Open all year. Eight guest rooms with private baths. Rates: $85 per room, except for 2 bridal suites $125 and $145. Includes full breakfast of fresh farmers' eggs. Children 6 and over welcome; no pets; no smoking; Polish and Russian spoken; Visa/MasterCard. Many fine restaurants in area, which is noted for Alpine skiing, fall foliage, and the lake and countryside seen in the film *On Golden Pond.*

DIRECTIONS: take exit 24 from I-93 onto Rte. 25/3 into Ashland and left on Highland to inn.

CRAB APPLE INN

With an English country garden

Crab Apple Inn is charming—from its well-preserved doorway fan to its babbling brook. White trim and black shutters complement the 1835 brick Federal building and the white picket fence that encloses the tidy house and its brilliantly colored English country garden.

Two cheery third-floor rooms boast the best view, overlooking most of the inn's two-and-a-half acres and Crosby Mountain. Yet every guest gets something special: an arched canopy bed, a hand-carved sleigh bed, a brass bed. Intimate and cozy, the household harbors warmth and hospitality.

The inn's library offers a variety of periodicals and books, and all the public rooms are tastefully furnished in a traditional style.

This is indeed snow country, the gateway to the White Mountains. Polar Caves is one mile down the road, and Waterville Valley and Tenney Mountain, minutes away.

Warm weather enthusiasts can wade in nearby Newfound Lake or relax on the brick patio, sipping iced tea by the French doors, with candy and fresh fruit available. Breakfasts, whether indoors or *al fresco*, feature delicious home-cooked fare such as lemon ricotta pancakes with sautéed apples, featherbed eggs, or delicate crêpes with blueberry sauce.

Christine DeCamp, the affable innkeeper, attends to the small details that makes life more enjoyable when on the road—leaving terry cloth robes for those guests in rooms with shared baths and offering wine or tea and snacks in the afternoon.

An award-winning sign.

CRAB APPLE INN. Rte. 25, Box 188, Plymouth, NH 03264; (603) 536-4476; Christine DeCamp, keeper. Open all year. Five guestrooms, 3 with private baths and air conditioning. Rates: $60 to $85, including a gourmet breakfast. Children over 12 welcome; no pets; no smoking; MasterCard/Visa. All-season recreation in area; antiquing. Good restaurants nearby.

DIRECTIONS: from I-93, take exit 26 and head west on Rte. 25. The inn is 4 miles from the interstate on the left.

BENJAMIN PRESCOTT INN

American history

Built as a hostelry by Colonel Benjamin Prescott, a hero of the Battle of Bunker Hill, this inn is a footnote in the pages of American history. Each room bears the name of a Prescott family member.

Barry and Jan Miller have comfortably furnished the inn and filled it with all manner of interesting collectibles. Barry inherited his grandfather's collection of sand from around the world, and there are ship models (assembled by Barry) including the *Eagle*, an 1850s Maine schooner. Also displayed are framed groupings of vintage postcards, as well as rug beaters, trolley tokens, and antique children's clothing arranged like a Smithsonian exhibit.

The John Adams attic suite on the third floor is well worth the steep climb. Its spacious bedchamber, with two built-in sleeping alcoves and adjoining sitting room (with kitchen, stereo facilities, and scenic balcony), are fashioned out of fantasy.

What the hosts have not been able to do is create the setting, but beautiful New Hampshire provides that. The house backs out onto a vast seven-hundred acre pastoral dairy farm with a view of the farmer driving his hay wagon to and from the barn.

Cross-country and alpine skiing are minutes away, and the renowned Peterborough Players perform top-rated summer stock. Historic Jaffrey Center is a delightful colonial village brimming with history.

Barry, formerly a hotel manager, is the perfect host. And Jan's bedside chocolate truffles cannot be described in mere words.

THE BENJAMIN PRESCOTT INN. Rte. 124, Jaffrey, NH 03452; (603) 532-6637 (same for Fax); Barry and Janice Miller, owners. Open all year. Ten rooms with ceiling fans, including 2 suites with air conditioning, all with private baths. Rates: $60 to $130 per room or suite, including full breakfast. Children 10 and over welcome; no pets; smoking in common rooms only; Visa/MasterCard/American Express. Recommended dining at LataCarta, Boiler House, Del Rossi. See the Cathedral of the Pines and Mt. Monadnock.

DIRECTIONS: on Rte. 124 east of Jaffrey 2.3 miles.

All the rooms are different.

THE CHASE HOUSE

A famous banker's birthplace

Born in 1808, Salmon P. Chase spent the first decade of his life in the village of Cornish, New Hampshire. By the age of eleven he was sent to Ohio to live with his uncle, an Episcopal bishop, but in time Chase returned to New Hampshire to attend Dartmouth College. Eventually he was elected to the United States Senate, and after six years was elected to two terms as Ohio's governor, after which he returned to Washington and the Senate. From there, this remarkable American went on to serve Abraham Lincoln as Secretary of the Treasury, and soon thereafter was appointed Chief Justice of the United States, where he served until his death in 1873. In his lifetime he was a tireless anti-slavery spokesman; founded the Republican Party; had his picture engraved on the $10,000 bill; and gave his name to the Chase Manhattan Bank.

Chase's birthplace, one of the finest homes in this tiny Connecticut River valley village, has been meticulously restored as a bed and breakfast inn by Peter Burling, an attorney and a member of Cornish's town planning board. He commissioned the talents of experienced restoration experts, who thoroughly and carefully pieced together the checkered history of the house.

The result is a stunning, early Federal house that sits on the banks of the river, surrounded by stately shade trees. The furnishings throughout are elegant, comfortable, and simple, and they enhance one's enjoyment of the home's lovely architectural detail.

The full breakfast that is served each morning prepares one for exploring the wooded New England countryside. The Chase House is centrally located nearby Hanover and Dartmouth College, as well as the sophisticated shops and restaurants of Woodstock, Vermont.

THE CHASE HOUSE. RR 2, Box 909, Cornish, NH 03745; (800) 401-9455, (603) 675-5391, Fax (603) 675-5010; Bill and Barbara Lewis, owners. Open all year except for Nov. and Dec. Eight rooms, 7 with private baths, 1 sharing. Rates: $85 to $115, with full breakfast. Children over 12 welcome; no pets; no smoking; Visa/MasterCard. Canoeing, hiking, cross country skiing.

DIRECTIONS: from I-91 take Ascutney exit 8 across Connecticut River, turn north on Rte. 12A for 4 miles to inn.

High ceilings make for grand spaces.

AMOS A. PARKER HOUSE

The place to get away from it all

If wandering off the beaten track is your idea of the perfect getaway, the southwest corner of New Hampshire beckons. Visitors to the area come to escape the rat race and to get in touch with life's essentials. The area is richly blessed with sparkling lakes, ponds, and streams; groves of rhododendron that burst into bloom each summer; and maple trees that glow in the autumn and produce sweet syrup in early spring. The region is dominated by Mount Monadnock, which over the years has inspired such artists as Emerson, Kipling, and Kilmer. Thoreau climbed to the summit three times, and the mountain was a constant companion during his solitary sojourn on Walden Pond.

Such relaxed and gentle surroundings are complemented by the historic Amos A. Parker House.

The Great Room, so-named because everyone exclaims, "What a great room!" when they first see it.

A stay at this colonial bed and breakfast inn is like visiting a favorite relative. Innkeeper Freda Houpt is the inn's genial host and she makes visitors feel a part of this fine old place. The earliest section of the house dates back to the mid-1700s, with an addition built in 1780. Freda has filled her home with comfortable furnishings that match the Federal period, museum quality orientals, and antiques. She is justifiably proud of her gardens and her lawn, which sweeps gently to an active beaver pond at the edge of the grass.

Besides the natural beauty of the area, visitors enjoy cultural events, such as plays and concerts, offered throughout the year. Also, the village of Fitzwilliam (which, for trivia buffs, is the only town in the United States bearing that name), as well as the surrounding countryside, is well-known for the quality of its antiques and crafts shops.

AMOS A. PARKER HOUSE. Box 202, Rte. 119, Fitzwilliam, NH 03447; (603) 585-6540; Freda B. Houpt, proprietor. Open all year. Four rooms, including 2 suites, all with private baths. Rates: $70 to $85 with full breakfast. Children over 10 welcome; no pets; no smoking; no credit cards. Inn has beautiful gardens. Canoeing, golf, tennis, hiking, biking. Country inn dining nearby.

DIRECTIONS: from I-91 take exit 28A to Rte. 10 north to Rte. 119 east. From Boston take Rte. 2 west to Rte. 140 north to Rte. 12 north to Rte. 119 west.

Chauncy's Room.

HANNAH DAVIS HOUSE

Relax and enjoy the charm

This beautifully restored 1820 clapboard house is a frequent stop for antiques buyers browsing the area's shops. It's also a fine place to relax and enjoy the charm of the house and its owners, Kaye and Mike Terpstra.

Situated in the heart of the Manadnock region of southern New Hampshire, just down the road from the town common of Fitzwilliam, the Federal-style house offers six bedrooms, ranging from suites to smaller, cozy rooms. One suite has a bedroom in a loft perched above a sitting room. Chauncey's Room has a high, queen-sized antique iron bed, a wood-burning fireplace and bold red floral wallpaper. There is an extra twin-sized bed in the room.

Several common rooms are available for guests. A small living room with a piano is situated off one of two dining rooms. The front dining room is dominated by an antique table sitting on a hooked

Left below, the breakfast room.

rug. A second dining room, just off the kitchen, is fronted with the original fireplace, complete with a baking oven. Hand-hewn oak beams run the length of the ceiling. Much of the original hand-forged iron-work—door latches, hinges, and handles—has been preserved.

Adjacent to the dining room is a bank of sliding glass doors that open out onto an elevated screened porch that wraps around the house. The porch overlooks herb, vegetable, and flower gardens and a wooded bog where herons hunt and songbirds greet the morning. A pair of binoculars and bird books can be found on a table next to the porch swing.

Breakfast is an event, with a menu that includes coffee and tea, homemade granola and applesauce, Kaye's cinnamon-raisin bread, cantaloupe and grapes, spanikopita, scrambled eggs, country ham, and fresh green beans.

HANNAH DAVIS HOUSE. 186 Depot Rd., Fitzwilliam, NH 03447; (603) 585-3344; Kaye and Mike Terpstra, owners. Open all year. Six rooms, all with private baths. Rates: $60 to $95, including breakfast. Children welcome; no pets, no smoking indoors; Visa/MasterCard/Discover. Antiques shopping, hiking, mountain climbing, golf, skiing, pond swimming.

DIRECTIONS: from Boston take Rte. 2 west to Rte. 140 north to Rte. 12 north to Rte. 119 west (which is Depot Rd.).

VERMONT

Left, the luxuriously furnished guest rooms are brilliantly decorated. Above, the main house.

SWIFT HOUSE INN

Genuinely luxurious

Swift House is sited impressively in a park-like setting of sweeping lawns, stately trees, and colorful flower gardens.

The entire main floor houses fruitwood-paneled reception rooms for guests' use. There is a formal sitting room, relaxing parlor, intimate bar, and an inviting screened-in porch—light and airy with white wicker furnishings—that looks out on the spacious grounds.

Five guest rooms on the second floor are superbly furnished, each being more inviting than the last. The Addison Room is decorated in pink and white wallpaper, with white wicker furniture and an ornate white iron bed. But then the Swift Room has a lovely canopied bed, and a huge bathroom with a claw-footed tub, separate stall shower, and private sun deck.

All this, however, describes only one third of the inn. Though everyone eats breakfast at the main house, across the street is the Gate House, with another five luxurious guest rooms and sitting rooms of its own. And beyond the circular driveway is the Carriage House, which was recently renovated into five guest rooms and aromatic cedar sauna, steam room, and showers.

Andrea and John Nelson bought the estate in 1985, with plans to convert it to an inn. Their consummate taste prevails throughout, and they have proven themselves masters of the ancient and noble art of innkeeping.

The previous owner was the daughter of John W. Stewart, a former Governor of Vermont, who bought the original house in 1875 from its builder, Judge Samuel Swift. Stewart's daughter lived there for 105 years, until her death in 1981 at the age of 110.

SWIFT HOUSE INN AND GATEHOUSE. 25 Stewart Lane, Middlebury, VT 05753; (802) 388-9925, Fax (802) 388-9927; Andrea and John Nelson, owners. Open all year. Fifteen guest rooms in Swift House and Gate House and 6 rooms in Carriage House, all with private baths and air conditioning. Rates: $90 to $165 per room, including continental breakfast. Children welcome; no pets; smoking in designated rooms only; all major credit cards.

DIRECTIONS: from south stay on Rte. 7 through Middlebury past Middlebury Inn a few blocks and turn right on Stewart Lane, which intersects Rte. 7 near Mobil station.

The breakfast room.

THE INN AT ROUND BARN FARM

A perfect 10

The Inn at Round Barn Farm is a superlative combination of unique and historic architecture, beautifully landscaped grounds, cultural and recreational opportunities, and luxurious accommodations.

The architectural centerpiece is the Joslyn Round Barn, built in 1910 by dairy farmer Clem Joslyn. When Jack and Doreen Simko bought the property in 1986, the barn—one of only eight round barns remaining in Vermont—was disintegrating. But a two-year restoration project has beautifully restored the building, now used for weddings, concerts, business conferences, and art exhibits. The need for a water supply for the sprinkler system has resulted in a sixty-foot lap pool on the bottom floor of the barn.

The adjacent farmhouse has eleven guest rooms, all uniquely decorated. The Dana Room is one of the four new luxurious rooms added by the conversion of the carriage barn. This second-floor open-raftered room features a queen-sized white chiffon-canopied bed, wicker fainting couch, polished black granite fireplace, and views of the mountains. The glass-enclosed bath also functions as a steamshower. There are additional amenities like terry cloth robes and magnifying mirrors by the bathroom sink.

A ground-level library with a fireplace offers a wide selection of Vermont and New England coffee table books. A decanter of sherry is always set out. A basement game room boasts a pool table and television/VCR with a selection of movies. Breakfast is served in a long airy dining room with windows running the length of two walls. The dining room opens out onto a terraced patio overlooking the grounds.

The Simkos' earlier career as horticulturists is evidenced in the eighty-five acres of landscaped grounds that surround the farm. The terraced lawn rolls down to ponds bordered with flowering plants and afloat with water lilies. Trellised fruit trees frame the buildings. Interspersed throughout the grounds are whimsical sculptures, many made from discarded farm implements.

THE INN AT ROUND BARN FARM. East Warren Rd., Waitsfield, VT 05673; (802) 496-2276; Jack and Doreen Simko, owners. Open all year. Eleven rooms, all with private baths. Rates: $100 to $185 (minus $10 for singles), including breakfast. Children over 15 accepted; no pets; no smoking; Visa/MasterCard. Nordic ski resort on grounds, Alpine skiing, hiking.

DIRECTIONS: from Waitsfield turn off Rte. 100 at Bridge St., travel through covered bridge and bear right at the fork onto East Warren Rd. Inn is one mile further on left.

Left, the Dana Room, newly converted in the Carriage Barn.

Overleaf, a Mozart concert is one of the cultural attractions.

SHOREHAM INN AND COUNTRY STORE

A tiny town on Lake Champlain

Surrounded by apple orchards and dairy farms, and bordered on one side by Lake Champlain's sinuous tail, the Shoreham Inn and its adjoining Country Store form the heart of tiny Shoreham, Vermont. The inn's atmosphere, reflecting its beautiful setting and kind proprietors, is warm, gentle, and welcoming.

Built in 1799 as a public house, it allows today's inngoers to walk the same wooden floorboards that its first visitors trod. These wide planks are partially hidden by lustrous old area rugs and an irregular collection of antiques—none matches, but all work together—that please the eye and comfort the spirit.

Cleo and Fred Alter love original art, a taste fully developed during the days they worked together in printing and graphic design, and they exercise this love by showing the work of gifted local artists. Not a gallery per se, the inn doesn't sell work but the Alters do take pleasure in sharing beautiful things with others.

Breakfast is low-keyed. On each table guests find a canning jar filled with granola, pitchers of milk and juice, local honey and preserves, muffins or scones, and cheese. Since this is apple country, Cleo always serves the fruit in one form or another. Glass cookie jars in the center of each large dining table are always stocked with homebaked sweets for snackers.

The Country Store, just next to the inn, supplies everything from magazines and groceries to hardware and wine. The Alters operate a small delicatessen in back, where you can order a pizza or sandwiches and salads. Picnic tables on the village green beckon on a summer day.

SHOREHAM INN AND COUNTRY STORE. Shoreham, VT 05770; (800) 255-5081, (802) 897-5081; Cleo and Fred Alter, hosts. Built as an inn in 1799, the Shoreham served as a way station for floating railroad bridge and ferry across Lake Champlain. Open all year except mid-Oct. to mid-Nov. Eleven guest rooms, some accommodating four people, shared baths. Rates: $50 single, $80 double, including country breakfast. Children welcome; no pets; no smoking; no credit cards. Area offers aquatic sports, museums, Ft. Ticonderoga, Morgan horse farm. Daily boat trips on lake.

DIRECTIONS: inn is 12 miles southwest of Middlebury. Follow Rte. 22A from Fairhaven to Rte. 74 west. From Burlington, take 7 south to 22A at Vergennes, then take 74 west into Shoreham. Ticonderoga ferry operates to and from Shoreham.

SHIRE INN

Where guests come to relax

One hour from Burlington and halfway between Boston and Montreal, the Shire Inn affords comfort and elegant surroundings for guests traveling through central Vermont.

Enclosed by a white picket fence, the house is constructed of handsome Vermont brick with a granite arch curving gracefully over its front door. Spring and summer gardens add color and fragrance; a wooden bridge stands behind the inn and the White River flows past it.

Six distinct guest rooms, all named for counties in Vermont, are furnished with period antiques. Four of them having working fireplaces. All of the bedsteads are dressed with country bedspreads and ample comforters and a generous supply of books and magazines is provided in all rooms.

A sumptuous full breakfast is served. Favorite entrées include fresh herb omelets with Vermont cheddar cheese, blueberry pancakes, and French toast.

Dinners are served during the week by reservation. A minimum two-night weekend includes one five-course dinner which might feature baked salmon filet, roast breast of duck with Chambord sauce, or veal scallopine with wild rice and apricots served with shitake mushroom sauce.

Cross-country skiing in Chelsea, downhill skiing in Barnard, swimming and boating on Lake Fairlee, theater, art galleries, and restaurants in nearby Woodstock and Montpelier make the Shire an inn for all seasons.

THE SHIRE INN, P.O. Box 37, Main St., Chelsea, VT 05038; (800) 441-6908, (802) 685-3031; Jay and Karen Keller, innkeepers. Open all year. Federal-style brick house built in 1832. Six guest rooms, all with private baths, four with working fireplaces. Rates: $86 to $110 double, depending on season. MAP $140 to $175. Delicious full breakfast included. Minimum two night weekend including one dinner. Children over 6 welcome; no pets; no smoking; Visa/MasterCard/Discover. Cross-country skiing (skis available at no extra charge), hiking, antiquing, bicycles available.

DIRECTIONS: from I-89 take the Sharon exit (exit 2) to Rte. 14 to S. Royalton, to Rte. 110 north to Chelsea. From I-91, take the Thetford exit (exit 14) to Rte. 113 north to Chelsea. The inn is on the village's main road, on the left.

The Josephine Room is exquisitely detailed.

THE JACKSON HOUSE AT WOODSTOCK

Elegant décor

The one hundred-year-old Jackson House is as friendly and warm as it is elegant. Although it has hosted travelers for the last fifty years, it was ony in 1984 that it became one of the most exquisitely furnished inns in Vermont, when Bruce McIlveen and Jack Foster took it in hand.

With consummate taste and the sensitive appreciation of connoisseurs, they have created ten guest rooms, each singularly fashioned, and all a memorable experience for guests.

We can mention only a few, the first being the Gloria Swanson Room, named after her because she stayed there. It is all done in birds-eye and curly maple—floors, bedstead, picture frames, and furniture—with a lemon, green, and white color scheme. The Mary T. Lincoln Room is High Victorian, with a great carved double bed, and an ornately tufted, green-upholstered occasional chair.

A full breakfast could consist of fresh fruit compôte with peach schnapps, Santa Fe omelets, rosemary potatoes, broccoli with hollandaise, and homemade scones and muffins.

A newly built spa includes weights, a treadmill, and a steam room. There is a big-screen TV and an extensive film library.

THE JACKSON HOUSE AT WOODSTOCK. Rte. 4 West, Woodstock, VT 05091; (802) 457-2065 (same for Fax); Jack D. Foster and Bruce McIlveen, hosts. Open all year. Twelve guest rooms, including 2 suites, all with private baths. Rates: $135 to $250, including full breakfast and evening cocktail hour. Children over 14 welcome; no pets; no smoking; no credit cards. Robert Trent Jones golf course, tennis in area. French touring bikes available down the street.

DIRECTIONS: 1½ miles west of Woodstock Village on Rte. 4.

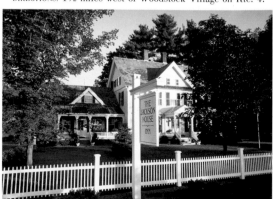

CHARLES A. PARKER PHOTOGRAPH

QUECHEE BED & BREAKFAST

Overlooking the Quechee Gorge

From the bunches of dried herbs and flowers hanging from the rafters, to the stencilled curtains, braided rugs, and hand-crafted wreaths, Susan Kaduboski has recreated an album of rooms from the pages of *Country Living*.

The Kaduboskis rescued an old post-and-beam colonial farm house and turned it into a charming bed and breakfast that resounds with special touches: a vintage sled coffee table festooned with plants, a graceful tapestry couch, plenty of family treasures, and an abundant dose of floral motifs.

Entering the house from the front, you can hardly anticipate the awesome view that awaits you. From windows at the rear of the inn, you suddenly discover that you are perched atop the Quechee Gorge, so aptly dubbed the "Grand Canyon of the East."

Outdoor tables and chairs provide excellent vantage points for viewing this beautiful section of the Ottaquechee River.

Guest rooms are all singular, with an assortment of pretty wallpapers, rice-carved four-posters, and sleigh beds on wide pine floorboards or hardwood floors. Some of the rooms offer spectacular views. Although the inn is on Route 4, hemlocks and woodpiles are useful as baffling, and colorful flower beds lap up to the windows.

The guest book is filled with rave reviews about the food served in the charming breakfast room. Perfectly scrambled eggs with chives, Vermont smoked meats, waffles done to a turn, and Susan's special French toast seem to be favorites.

You can walk over a covered bridge to the village of Quechee in a matter of minutes. Be sure to visit Simon Pearce, a mill converted into a store and restaurant, where you can shop for tableware, enjoy a meal, and watch glass-blowing artisans.

QUECHEE BED & BREAKFAST. 753 Woodstock Rd. (Rte. 4), P.O. Box 0080, Quechee, VT 05059; (802) 295-1776; Susan and Ken Kaduboski, owners. Open all year. Eight guest rooms with private baths and air conditioning. Rates: $95 to $135 per room, including full breakfast. No children; no pets; no smoking; Spanish spoken; Visa/MasterCard. Overlooks town of Quechee, with its shops, restaurants, crafts center, and glass works; nearby to Woodstock, one of America's most charming upscale villages.

DIRECTIONS: from west, exit 1 off I-89 to Rte. 4 west for 4 ½ miles. Watch for sign on right.

A gorgeous stone house in a park-like Vermont setting.

GREYSTONE

Rustic charm in horse country

Connie Miller transformed this 1830 stone house, that had once been a shoe factory, into a charming bed and breakfast, with lilac bushes and lavender plantings in front. Just down the way is the main street of Reading, with its library, school, town hall, church, and farmers' market—a picture-postcard town of six hundred souls.

This is horse country, home to the venerable Green Mountain Horse Association, and people from all over descend upon this area to ride. It is commonplace to see riders on the country roads, trails, and mountain tops. Ms. Miller herself is a seasoned rider, and her riding boots, and at times her saddle, are in the entryway of the house.

The Greystone's guest rooms are charming. One has a peach floral canopied bed with matching wallpaper and drapes. Another is papered in blue flowers, has a sitting room, and overlooks a mani-

cured lawn and gentle mountains. The third floor suite has wide floorboards, comfortable furnishings, skylights—and is a bit closer to heaven. All of the furnishings are Connie's, gathered on trips and from "past lives." There are also personal keepsakes, including drawings and photos of horses and riders, and an old sepia photograph of Connie as a child on her very first ride.

The parlor is warm and inviting, with its wood-burning stove, yellow wainscoting, blue trim, and floral wallpaper. Cows at a nearby dairy farm may be glimpsed from the parlor windows, and in autumn each window reveals a kaleidoscope of fall colors.

For non-riding spouses or friends, there is fishing on the grounds and swimming at a local swimming hole. There are plenty of antiques shops and auctions, and the town of Woodstock, with its restaurants and shops, is just a short distance away. Facilities at the Woodstock Inn include tennis courts, a pool, and an eighteen-hole golf course.

GREYSTONE. Rte. 106, Reading, VT 05062; (mailing address, P.O. Box 305, South Woodstock, VT 05071); (802) 484-7200 (same for Fax); Constance Hughes Miller, owner. Open all year. Three guest rooms with private and semi-private baths and one suite with private bath. Rates: $75 to $120 double, including full breakfast. Inquire about children; no pets; no smoking; no credit cards (personal checks accepted). Fine gourmet dining nearby.

DIRECTIONS: on Rte. 106, 10 miles south of Woodstock. Call for directions.

The wood paneled staircase, laden with teddy bears.

HUGGING BEAR INN

The healing power of Teddy Bears

The warm spirit of the Hugging Bear embraces one and all who pass through its doors. Georgette Thomas came to innkeeping from a caring career as a counselor with a degree in social work. When she discovered an article in *Prevention* magazine touting the healing power of teddy bears, she knew she had found the perfect theme for this rambling, Queen Anne Victorian bed and breakfast inn, which sits on the main street of historic Chester, Vermont.

Teddy bears are found in every nook and cranny of the inn. They play the piano, peek out from potted plants, climb the lovely Victorian staircase, and perch atop each bed. Besides the inn, the Hugging Bear Shoppe, located in the back, is dedicated to the irresistible charms of the teddy bear.

Georgette's son, Paul, a wildlife artist and sculptor, and his wife, Diane, help out with the innkeeping. Because the Thomases are sensitive to the difficulties of parents traveling with children, they welcome families with open arms. Children are encouraged to choose the teddy bears of their choice to sleep with at night, and occasionally they may borrow favorites from the shop, as long as they promise to return them "to work" by 8 A.M. But it isn't strictly children who are moved by this colorful menagerie of huggable creatures. The Thomases report that a majority of adults who pass through their inn fall under the spell of teddy bear power.

THE HUGGING BEAR INN & SHOPPE. Main Street, Box 32, Chester, VT 05143; (800) 325-0519, (802) 875-2412; Georgette, Paul, and Diane Thomas, hosts. Open all year except for Christmas. Six rooms with private baths. Rates: $55 to $65 single, $75 to $95 double, children under 14 $10, over 14 $20 extra, with full breakfast and afternoon cheese, crackers, and cider. Children welcome; inquire about pets; no smoking; all credit cards accepted. Four-room bear shop. Hugging teddy bears encouraged. Badminton, volleyball, croquet on premises. Antiquing, flea markets, auctions, biking, golf, tennis, and skiing nearby. A special event occurs on the second weekend of December, when the town celebrates a Victorian Christmas. Lighting trees, caroling, and wearing Victorian costumes are among the colorful activities. The inn provides period costumes for guests to wear to a reception for Santa Claus, who arrives in a horse drawn carriage or sled, snow permitting.

DIRECTIONS: located on the main street of Chester, Vermont.

The inn at dusk, sitting serenely in the Vermont countryside.

MADRIGAL INN

Across
a covered bridge

Madrigal Inn is unique in being a brand-new house built specifically as a bed and breakfast inn. Situated on a meadow and surrounded by hundreds of acres of forest, the inn is reached by crossing the Williams River on a covered bridge. The inn sits above the river and the railway used by the Green Mountains Flyer tour train.

Ray and Nancy Dressler finished construction of the inn on Christmas Eve, 1992, after Ray retired from thirty-six years—and twenty-two interstate and international transfers—as a Navy chaplain. They designed and oversaw construction of the post-and-beam, 13,000-square-foot house. The house is dominated by a common room with a cathedral ceiling and arched windows rising to a peak. A large loft overhead serves as a library and conference room. It boasts a fireplace and windows facing across the backyard to the forest.

Downstairs, opposite the central fireplace, a wood-paneled dining room holds several tables, providing

Left, the stunning proportions of the Common Room.

for either group or individual dining. Breakfast specialties are French toast with maple syrup, fruit, and muffins.

The eleven bedrooms, situated on three floors of the house, are individually decorated. The furnishings range from ruffled canopied beds to more simple Shaker-inspired beds and furniture. All beds have down comforters, and rollaways are available. With room for thirty guests, Madrigal Inn hosts weddings and business conferences. And the Dresslers have established a chamber music series at the inn, with performances by musicians from the Portland Symphony Orchestra and other groups, on the second Sunday of every month. The concert is limited to thirty-five people, and guests attend free. Each concert is followed with a dinner served in the inn's dining room.

The Dresslers have built a pond next to the inn which is used for swimming. There is also a small gift shop which sells crafts by local artisans.

THE MADRIGAL INN and FINE ARTS CENTER. 61 Williams River Rd., Chester, VT 05143; (800) 854-2208; Ray and Nancy Dressler, owners. Open all year. Eleven rooms, all with private baths. Rates: $65 single, $90 double including breakfast. Children accepted; no pets; no smoking; Visa/MasterCard/American Express/Discover. Boating, fishing, 5 kilometer hiking and cross-country skiing on grounds, pond for swimming, monthly chamber music concerts.

DIRECTIONS: off Rte. 103, four miles west of I-91. Turn at Brockways Mills Rd., cross covered bridge and proceed to inn.

All the guest rooms have Jacuzzis; the bubble bath is an added touch.

INN VICTORIA

Tea-time is the day's highlight

Inn Victoria is probably better known for its afternoon tea than its breakfasts. There's nothing shabby about breakfasts here, where eggs Benedict, home-baked coffee cake, and muffins are served in a formal dining room agleam with crystal and silver.

But, in keeping with the Victorian British theme, owners K.C. and Tom Lanagan have established tea-time as the social highlight of the day. There's a variety of top hats, derbies, and feathered head-dresses available for guests to wear to really get into the mood. K.C. also has a one-room shop next door, where she sells elegant china teapots. The parlor and the rest of the three-story yellow brick house are appointed in ultra-Victorian style, replete with fainting couches. The parlor is decorated with a rose

Left above, the inn, a mansard-roofed architectural gem. Below, the elegant sitting room/parlor.

Breakfast is served in the dining room.

Crystal and silver service in the dining room.

colored carpet and wallpaper. Beautifully uphol-stered formal chairs and sofas surround the gas fire-place.

Inn Victoria has allowed for improvements on the Victorian era by equipping all the rooms with Jacuzzi tubs. The inn has seven bedrooms, five with queen-sized beds and two with double beds. Elaborately carved walnut headboards and potted flowers are the standard.

Inn Victoria is set on the green—an open pedes-trian section of Chester housing art galleries, coffee shops, craft shops, and restaurants. A museum is across the street.

INN VICTORIA. On the Green, Chester, VT 05143; (800) 732-4288; K.C. and Tom Lanagan, owners. Open all year. Seven rooms, all with private baths. Rates: $85 to $125, including breakfast. Children accepted; no pets; no smoking; Visa/MasterCard/American Express. Skiing, antiques shopping, bicycle tours.

DIRECTIONS: located on the green in downtown Chester.

One of the elaborately carved headboards for which the guest rooms are noted.

SOUTH SHIRE INN

Special personality and comfort

Bennington, Vermont is a bustling New England village, tucked securely in a broad and handsome Green Mountain valley. The South Shire Inn, which sits at the edge of the handsome residential district, is perfectly situated between historic Old Bennington, with its famous Battle Monument, Old First Church, and Old Burying Ground (resting place of poet Robert Frost) and the shops and restaurants that cluster at the village center.

The house dates back to the late 1800s, when Bennington's prominent Graves family built a compound of five adjoining mansions to accommodate the burgeoning clan. No expense was spared when they raised Louis Graves' Queen Anne Victorian home, and today this solid and spacious mansion serves as Bennington's finest bed and breakfast inn.

Owned by Pat and Winnie Raffaele, the South Shire Inn is striking and handsome. Of special note on the first floor is the very grand library, paneled with lustrous Honduran mahogany and outfitted with a working, tile-faced fireplace and built-in, leaded glass bookcases. The adjoining breakfast room is so encrusted with rococo plaster friezes it could put a wedding cake to shame.

One bedroom is found on the inn's first floor and the remainder are located upstairs, on the second and third floors. Each has its own special comfort and personality. Several spacious chambers come complete with working fireplaces.

Great care and thought went into restoring and furnishing the inn, which adds to the sense of solidity and "rightness" about the place. The turn-of-the-century carriage barn has recently been renovated into luxurious guest rooms, with fireplaces and Jacuzzi baths.

THE SOUTH SHIRE INN, 124 Elm Street, Bennington, VT 05201; (802) 447-3839, Fax (802) 442-3547; Tim and Kristina Mast, innkeepers. Open all year. Nine rooms with private baths, 7 with fireplaces, 4 with Jacuzzis. Rates: $90 to $135, varying seasonally. Children over 10 welcome; no pets; no smoking; Visa/MasterCard/American Express. State-of-the-art facilities available for conferences. Fishing, golf, hiking, antiquing, museums, outlet stores in area. Many restaurants for dining.

DIRECTIONS: take Elm St. off Rte. 7 between Jefferson and Dewey.

The back garden, where Norman Rockwell's studio is located.

THE INN ON COVERED BRIDGE GREEN

Norman Rockwell slept here

Norman Rockwell came to Arlington, Vermont, when he was forty-six years old, inspired by the beautiful countryside and the people who lived there—of whom he said ". . . the sincere, honest, homespun types that I love to paint." From 1941 to 1954, he lived in the house that is now The Inn on Covered Bridge, painting his war-years pictures in the studio behind. *The Country Doctor, Christmas Homecoming, First Day at School* were among these paintings, and many of the townsfolk were his models.

Anne and Rob Weber, Americans who lived in England, and later in a Scottish castle, have bought and assumed stewardship of the Rockwell house. They brought sets of antique furniture, armoires, washstands, and carpets from Europe to furnish the two-hundred-year-old farmhouse, where Rockwell's visitors included his good friend, Grandma Moses.

Across the way from the inn's front porch is the grassy lawn where Ethan Allen drilled his Green Mountain Boys, whom he led in the surprise attack to capture the British-held Fort Ticonderoga. There is a pavilion on the green, where Rockwell and his neighbors danced on Saturday night, and beyond that, a classic Vermont covered bridge from which the inn takes its name.

Nearby flows the Batten Kill River, one of America's finest trout streams. A stroll along River Road provides panoramic views of neighboring farms and meadows, and there are superb hiking trails on Stratton Mountain. Three of the finest summer stock theaters are just a half hour away as is *Hildene*, Robert Todd Lincoln's estate.

A gallery housed in an historic Arlington church displays Rockwell's *Saturday Evening Post* covers, illustrations, and ads. You get the uncanny feeling that people you see there today—at the gas station, at the general store, in the churchyard—are the very same people he drew for magazine covers a generation ago.

THE INN ON COVERED BRIDGE GREEN. RD 1, Box 3550, Arlington, VT 05250; (800) 726-9480, (802) 375-9489, Fax (802) 375-1208; Anne and Ron Weber, owners. Open all year. Five guest rooms in inn plus Norman Rockwell's studio in garden, all with private baths. Rates: $110 to $145 double, $133 to $333.50 for entire studio (sleeps 6). Includes full breakfast. Well-mannered children welcome; no pets; no smoking; no credit cards. Excellent dining in Arlington and East Arlington.

DIRECTIONS: from Rte. 7 in Arlington take Rte. 313 west at Arlington Inn for 4½ miles to red covered bridge.

1811 HOUSE

An upscale inn with a pub

For almost a century-and-a-half, Manchester has flourished as a vacation place and spa. Early visitors found its inns, taverns, beautiful countryside, and four miles of marble sidewalks a welcome escape from the city. Mary Todd Lincoln came here to rest from the tensions of the Civil War.

Franklin Orvis, a key figure in Manchester's growth, was an early hosteler and part of his original home is incorporated into the Equinox Hotel—a sprawling resort with a spa and golf course. The back of the 1811 House, with its magnificently tended flower gardens, looks out on the Equinox golf course and Bromley Mountain.

This is not just another inn. The groomed and elegant 1811 House is impeccable inside and out. An historic building, it is ideally situated next to the classic New England-spired church on the equally classic Manchester village green.

All of the rooms in the house are simple and lovely. The first-floor parlors and dining room are furnished with a collection of fine English antiques, crystal, and paintings of country scenes. Each of

A second floor guest room.

the ten bedrooms has a private bath, sports its own color scheme, and exudes its own personality.

In the center of the building there is an English pub with dartboard and fireplace. This fits well with Bruce Duff's passion for wine, and he is the consummate bar tender—an oenophile who metes out his superb wines measure-for-measure with his knowledge of the grape. Gardening, his other love, has bloomed in the terraced gardens, which overwhelm the senses with their color and fragrance.

Marny, who used to teach cooking, enjoys preparing a full gourmet breakfast that might include eggs Benedict, grilled mushrooms, succulent ham, bacon, scones, and an endless variety of pancakes. Along with freshly-squeezed juice or fresh fruit, the fare is presented on fine china and crystal.

These are special innkeepers who love sharing their passions with those lucky enough to be their guests.

1811 HOUSE. Manchester Village, VT 05254; (802) 362-1811, Fax (802) 362-2443; Bruce and Marny Duff, innkeepers. Excellent example of Federal architecture, which was long a famous summer resort in the 1800s. Open year-round. Fourteen guest rooms, private baths. Rates: $110 to $200 double. Full sit-down breakfast. No children under sixteen; no pets; no smoking; major credit cards. Small Scottish pub on premises (guests on honor system). Excellent dining in the area and occasional dinners served at the inn for guests. Hiking, fishing, tennis, golf, swimming, antiquing.

DIRECTIONS: Inn is in Manchester Village on the green, next to the Congregational Church (with spire).

MASSACHUSETTS

APPLEGATE

Luxurious elegance

Situated on six acres of beautifully landscaped grounds north of Lee in the Berkshire Mountains, Nancy and Rick Cannata's home is an elegant retreat in a peaceful rural setting. Past the iron gate and up the tree-lined driveway, one arrives at the portico, framed by tall white columns. An airy common room provides an area to gather around the fireplace, with a baby grand piano for the musically inclined.

A carved wooden staircase leads to six bedrooms appointed with antique beds and fine linens. Persian rugs cover the oak floors. A crystal decanter of brandy and a box of Belgian chocolates await guests in each room. A large screened porch runs the length of the house in the back, overlooking a swimming pool. Apple trees and a stone wall surround the pool.

Home-baked breads and rolls, quiches, fresh-squeezed orange juice, fruit, and rich coffee are served from 8 to 10 A.M. in a large dining room framed with windows that let in the morning sun. The Cannatas have created their own restaurant review guide: a journal in which guests are invited to review the restaurants where they dine. The guests pull no punches, with commentaries ranging from rave reviews to "all show, no go."

A golf course is across the road from Applegate, and bicycles are available to guests who wish to explore the winding roads. Many guests regularly stay at Applegate to attend concerts at nearby Tanglewood, with its numerous theatre and dance companies.

APPLEGATE. 279 W. Park St., Lee, MA 01238; (413) 243-4451; Nancy and Rick Cannata, owners. Open all year. Six rooms, all with private baths. Rates: $85 to $190 Nov. to May; $100 to $225, June to Aug; $100 to $210, Sept. to Oct., including full breakfast. Children over 12 accepted; no pets; no smoking indoors; Visa/MasterCard. Berkshires recreation, plus music, theater, and dance festivals; bicycles available.

DIRECTIONS: from I-90, go north on exit 2 to first stop sign; proceed ½ mile to Applegate on left.

The breakfast room.

A guest room.

Left above, the gracious living room. Below, the house backs on a garden and pool.

THE GABLES INN

A celebration of the Gilded Age

Back in 1899, when the writer Edith Wharton lived here, the house was known as Pine Acre, one of the original "cottages" built in Lenox by the literati of the late nineteenth century. Today the Gables Inn is a celebration of the Gilded Age, a veritable museum of Victorian art and culture.

Nineteenth-century paintings of fashionably dour men and women of significance look down on breakfasting guests in the dining room. A crystal chandelier hangs above the long dining table set with crystal and china. Adjacent to the parlor is Wharton's library, featuring many books by and about the author, best known for *The Age of Innocence* and *Ethan Frome*, a novel set in the village of Lenox.

Throughout the house, original oil paintings and photographs depicting life in turn-of-the-century Berkshires abound. Among the eighteen bedrooms in the Queen Anne-style home is the Presidents' Room, which displays one of the largest collections of presidential pictures, autographs and memorabilia. The Show Business Room is bedecked with memorabilia from theater and film, including highlights of innkeeper Frank Newton's own theatrical productions. The most popular room at the Gables is the Teddy Wharton Suite, a large room decorated in dark green and dominated by a king-sized bed framed with a carved walnut headboard. Many of the bedrooms have wood-burning fireplaces.

Out back, the lawn slopes down to a covered, heated swimming pool and adjacent tennis courts.

The Gables is a few minutes' walk from a variety

Left above, the Teddy Wharton Room. Below, the indoor pool and tennis court.

Victorian carpentry decorates the front entrance.

of restaurants, galleries and shops. Tanglewood, summer home of the Boston Symphony Orchestra, provides a full season of classical and contemporary concerts. Jacob's Pillow, America's oldest dance center, is also nearby.

THE GABLES INN. 103 Walker St., Route 183, Lenox, MA 01240; (413) 637-3416; Mary and Frank Newton, owners. Open all year. Eighteen rooms, all with private baths. Rates: $90 to $195, including breakfast. Children over 12 accepted; no pets; smoking allowed; Visa/MasterCard/Discover. Berkshires recreation plus Tanglewood, theater, dance.

DIRECTIONS: located at junction of Walker St. (Rte. 183) and Kemble St. From points south: Rte. 7 north through Stockbridge, bear left onto Route 7A to Lenox. From points west and east: Route 20 to Route 183 west to Lenox.

The dining room.

HAUS ANDREAS

Bed and breakfast with amenities

Haus Andreas, a full-service bed and breakfast, is a vacation in itself where hospitality and entertainment are the focus. Overlooking a pastoral view, the colonial mansion was built by a soldier of the American Revolution. During the summer of 1942, the estate became the residence of Queen Wilhelmina of the Netherlands and members of the royal family.

Continental breakfast is enhanced with a view that is truly inspiring—manicured lawns, birch trees, corn fields, and the mountains.

The formal, well-appointed bedrooms are clean and spare, with fussiness and embellishments kept to a minimum. Antiques in such a setting assume center spotlight.

Outdoors, tennis, croquet, and a heated swimming pool keep many guests busy; indoors there is an exercise room. The nine-hole golf course nearby attracts many visitors, and bicycles are available to guests who want to stray a little farther.

A delicious breakfast that might include scrambled eggs and bacon, seasonal pancakes, or baked French toast with fruit is served up on the Schenck's fine family china.

HAUS ANDREAS. 85 Stockbridge Road, Lee, MA 01238; (413) 243-3298; Sally and Ben Schenck, inn-keepers. Ten guest rooms, all with private baths, four with fireplaces; suites available. Rates: $60 to $250 depending on season and summer weekends 3 nights minimum stay; includes full breakfast. A 5% charge is added to the bill for the maids. Inquire about children and pets; all major credit cards. Heated swimming pool. Fine dining in area.
    DIRECTIONS: call for specific directions.

HAWTHORNE INN

A stimulating haven

In the mid-1970s artist Gregory Burch was attracted to Concord and to this house, which was large enough to contain his painting and sculpture studio as well as rooms for wayfarers. He and his wife Marilyn offer guests the comforts of an impeccably maintained and antiques-filled home. Gregory's soapstone bas-relief carvings and energetic paintings, and Marilyn's beautifully designed quilts contribute, along with books of poetry and art, and Mayan and Inca artifacts, to make the Hawthorne Inn a very stimulating haven.

HAWTHORNE INN. 462 Lexington Rd., Concord, MA 01742; (508) 369-5610, Fax (508) 287-4949; Gregory Burch and Marilyn Mudry, hosts. Charming inn on site steeped in American history. Open all year. Seven guest rooms with private baths, most air conditioned. Rates: $125 single, $160 double, $10 third person. Continental breakfast. All major credit cards; no pets; no smoking. Wide variety of restaurants within 10-minute drive. Equally wide variety of sports and spots of interest.

  DIRECTIONS: from Rte. 128-95, take exit 45 west for 3½ miles. Bear right at the single blinking light. Inn is one mile on left, across from "Wayside" (Hawthorne and Alcott home).

MERRELL TAVERN INN

Fine antiques in a stagecoach inn

Catering to travelers since the 1800s, the old Merrell Tavern has been painstakingly restored to its former glory by Charles and Faith Reynolds. It is now elegantly furnished with fine Sheraton and Heppelwhite antiques the Reynolds have collected over twenty-five years. Canopied, four-poster, and pencil-post bedsteads with deluxe mattresses, sought out for their exquisite comfort, ensure a pleasurable night's sleep. In the morning guests gather in the tavern for breakfast, which may feature Charles' special omelets, pancakes, and sausages, or perhaps a new find from a cookbook. A visit will reveal more treasures; there is not space here to do them justice.

MERRELL TAVERN INN. Rte. 102, South Lee, MA 01260; (413) 243-1794, Fax (413) 243-2669; Charles and Faith Reynolds, hosts. Closed Christmas Eve and Day. Nine guest rooms, 3 with fireplaces, all with private baths. Rates: $55 to $135 double, according to season and amenities, weekend packages available. All rates include full breakfast. Children welcome; no pets; Visa/MasterCard; no smoking.

  DIRECTIONS: exit Mass. Turnpike at Lee (exit 2) and follow Rte. 102 three miles toward Stockbridge.

Handmade quilts in the guest rooms.

GOLDBERRY'S B&B

Organic breakfasts

Breakfast at Goldberry's comes fresh from a cooperative farm to which owners Bev and Ray Scheer belong. The lemon ricotta pancakes with blueberry sauce and fresh spinach frittatas reflect a commitment to healthy, organic foods and an involvement with the progressive community of Williamstown.

The Scheers, both former school teachers, run a small, intimate bed and breakfast with three bedrooms, each with private bath. The white clapboard, two-story house was built in 1830 and in the late 1800s served as the Glen Female Seminary, a girls' school known to the then all-male Williams College students as the Glen-Fem-Sem. The guest rooms are furnished with antiques and queen-sized beds covered with handmade quilts. A small sitting room with a bank of windows makes a quiet place to read. A large common room is adjacent to the dining room. An elevated covered porch wraps around the back of the house, shaded by a large birch tree.

In keeping with their low-key approach, the Scheers have no sign advertising the home. Instead, whenever guests are expected, they hang a cow flag above the front door.

GOLDBERRY'S BED & BREAKFAST. 39 Cold Spring Rd., Williamstown, MA 01267; (413) 458-3935; Bev and Ray Scheer, owners. Open all year. Three rooms, all with private baths. Rates: $65 single, $80 double, including full breakfast. Children 3 and older accepted; no pets; no smoking; no credit cards. Williams College events, Clark Art Institute, Williamstown Theater Festival, hiking, skiing.

DIRECTIONS: from points south, go north on Rte. 7. Goldberry's is 4.1 miles from intersection of Rte. 43 and Rte. 7, on your left. From points west, go on Rte. 2, around the rotary in Williamstown, continue on Rte. 7 south. Goldberry's is third house on the right.

An 1878 Victorian.

WILLIAMSTOWN B&B

A Victorian house

Kim Rozell and Lucinda Edmonds left the fast-paced corporate world of Boston and now invite guests to relax with them in the beautiful and bucolic environs of Williamstown.

The expansive 1878 Victorian house is set back from the road on the edge of Williams College. In summer, guests may overhear actors from the Williamstown Theater Festival rehearsing in a nearby campus building. The immaculate house is decorated with antiques tastefully mixed with contemporary furniture. Each of the five bedrooms has clean, bright wallpaper, private baths, and unusual antiques. Bottles of Vermont spring water are set out for guests on antique marble-topped tables. Thick rugs cover the polished pine floors and love seats are set in alcoves in front of bay windows.

Breakfast is served in an open dining room that basks in the morning sun. Fresh bread and cereals are set out on the Hoosier kitchen cabinet, ("What every woman wants," notes the framed 1940s advertisement for the cabinet). Fresh rolls, waffles, pancakes, sausage, and eggs are regular breakfast fare.

The slate-roofed house has a covered porch in front where guests can relax on Adirondack chairs and view the landscaped grounds.

WILLIAMSTOWN BED & BREAKFAST. 30 Cold Spring Rd., Williamstown, MA 01267; (413) 458-9202; Kim Rozell and Lucinda Edmonds, owners. Open all year. Three rooms, all with private baths. Rates: $70 to $95, including full breakfast. No small children accepted; no pets; no smoking; no credit cards. Williams College events, Clark Art Institute, Williamstown Theater Festival, hiking, skiing.

DIRECTIONS: just off the traffic circle where Routes 2 and 7 join in Williamstown.

The guest rooms are individually and extravagantly decorated.

A CAMBRIDGE HOUSE

A fantasy of fabrics

Even the BBC has taken note of A Cambridge House, heralding it as "Boston's premier bed and breakfast." And no wonder!

Built in 1892, the Colonial Revival house is decorated with a flourish—with rolls of Victorian wallpapers and bolts of Waverly fabrics, oriental carpets, antique furniture, heavy draperies, and Chinese export bric-a-brac—looking very much the *Grande Dame* of Victoriana.

Through three owners the house has maintained its original integrity. Six working fireplaces, built-in corner cabinets, and beautiful hardwood floors are all original to the house. Owners Ellen Riley and Anthony Femmino bought the nine bedroom house as a residence, but after a few discerning guests were permitted to stay, a bed and breakfast was born.

Boston designers Dottie Scully and Tish Stagnone festooned the rooms with dainty floral and ribbon patterns, lavished with hundreds of yards of Waverly chintzes, damasks, and jacquards. Canopies, dust ruffles, swag curtains, and fresh floral bouquets create a romantic mood that resonates from room to room.

Breakfast is served in the parlor that connects to a luxurious den—and what a treat awaits you! A full breakfast is prepared by a talented chef, and may include delicate quiches, tasty omelets, fruit-topped waffles, and specially prepared low-fat sausage. All manner of complimentary goodies are available throughout the day.

A CAMBRIDGE HOUSE. 2218 Massachusetts Avenue, Cambridge, MA 02140-1836; (800) 232-9989, (617) 491-6300, Fax (617) 868-2848; Ellen Riley, Anthony Femmino, owners. Open all year. Eleven guest rooms with private baths in main house, 5 rooms sharing baths in carriage house. Rates: *main house* $109 to $225; *carriage house* $89 to $129, including chef-prepared full breakfast and special breakfast on Sundays. No children under 6; no pets; no smoking; All major credit cards. Many fine restaurants nearby.

DIRECTIONS: Massachusetts Avenue is a main thoroughfare running from Boston to Cambridge.

A breakfast to remember.

Afternoon tea at A CAMBRIDGE HOUSE *in Cambridge, Mass., outside of Boston.*

FAY FOTO

ON THE AVENUE

In the heart of Boston's Back Bay

A Victorian townhouse located in Boston's historic Back Bay is the home of a private club that offers its classic hospitality and quiet sophistication to selected guests through the Host Homes of Boston reservation service.

Steeped in history, the club has offered cultural and intellectual programs since 1890. Before that, it was the private home of the Robbins family, famous Boston clock makers.

The high-ceilinged guest rooms are attractively decorated with period antiques. The rooms with fireplaces also have private baths, whereas the other rooms share a bath for each two rooms. Breakfast is served in the formal dining room.

Within walking distance are the theater district, Beacon Hill, the Public Garden, Copley Place, Boston Common, and the smart boutiques, cafés, and galleries of Newberry Street, where Boston's elite like to meet.

ON THE AVENUE. Open all year. 4 doubles with twin beds and private baths; 5 singles, each sharing a bath with one other room. Rates: $65 to $95 single, $110 double; rollaways $25; including continental breakfast. Children 10 and over welcome; no pets; smoking in drawing room; Hungarian spoken; Visa/MasterCard/American Express. *Represented by Host Homes of Boston*, P.O. Box 117, Waban Branch, Boston, MA 02168; (617) 244-1308; Marcia Whittington.

DIRECTIONS: Maps mailed with confirmation. Some parking.

FAY FOTO

KIMBERLY GRANT PHOTOGRAPH

BEACON HILL

Stately guest rooms

Located on Boston's prestigious Beacon Hill and adjacent to the Massachusetts State House, the inn consists of two attached 1830s brick townhouses of twenty stately guest rooms. It is perfectly located for visiting the Boston Common, the Public Gardens, the Freedom Trail, and the Faneuil Hall/Quincy Market district.

The inn has been entirely renovated and charmingly decorated with beautiful period furnishings, and many guest rooms feature four-poster and canopied beds, decorative fireplaces, desks, private baths, and air conditioning. The rooms are striking, with floral patterns covering the walls and coordinated bed spreads and draperies complementing the tall windows that look out on the city.

An open kitchen is provided for self-serve breakfasts, and guests are always welcome to use the kitchen, the dining room, and the attractive parlors.

BEACON HILL. Attached 1830s brick townhouses with 20 guest rooms, 18 of which have private baths; there are 4 meeting rooms for conferences. Open all year. Rates: $89 single, $99 double, $10 additional guests. Includes stocked kitchen where you prepare your own full breakfast. Children welcome; no pets; no smoking; agency accepts all credit cards except Discover. Directions on reservation. *Represented by Bed and Breakfast Associates, Bay Colony Ltd., Boston, MA. (617) 449-5302.*

COPLEY SQUARE

A culinary treat

This restored 1863 five-story brick townhouse is set in the historic district adjacent to Boston's renowned Copley Square. It is within strolling distance of elegant restaurants, outdoor cafés, nearby theaters, the Hynes Convention Center, and bus and subway lines.

Sensitive attention to detail and gracious hospitality are the hallmark of this bed and breakfast. Each impeccable guest room offers uniquely decorative features including wide pine floors, bow windows, marble fireplaces, brass beds, armoires, full length paisley draperies, Chinese rugs, queen sized beds, and private baths. For those who would like them, four of the rooms provide a discreet galley kitchenette.

A generous full breakfast is served in the sun-filled penthouse breakfast room that is alive with skylights and views of the city. The host's culinary skills are showcased when he prepares and serves his perfectly turned blueberry buttermilk pancakes, French toast with tangy strawberry sauce, or old-fashioned scrambled eggs with succulent sausage. Those who prefer privacy are invited to enjoy a continental breakfast in their room.

COPLEY SQUARE. 1863 brick townhouse with 3 guest rooms with private baths. Open all year. Rates: $97 double, including full breakfast. Older children welcome; no pets; no smoking; agency accepts all credit cards. Directions on reservation. *Represented by Bed and Breakfast Associates, Bay Colony, Ltd., Boston, MA. (617) 449-5302.*

Innkeepers Jim and Caroline Lloyd on the porch of their bed and breakfast.

MOSTLY HALL

Cape Cod style plantation

Built in 1849 by a sea captain for his New Orleans bride, this inn is a Southern plantation-style home, perched majestically in a Cape Cod town. It received its unusual name when a visiting child walked in and marveled, "Why Mama, it's mostly hall!"

Indeed, the interior of the four-story bed and breakfast is dominated by its hallways and long, graceful staircases. The main floor features thirteen-foot ceilings and grand, full-length windows. Other architectural pleasures include a porch that wraps completely around all four sides of the inn, and a widow's walk. This cheerful, square little room, with its ten windows all around, is a favorite hideout for guests.

All of the six guest rooms occupy a corner of the inn, and feature queen-sized canopied beds. Like the spacious living room, with its Italian marble fireplace, they are elegantly decorated in a combination of antique and traditional furnishings. The home itself is set far back on a large lot, lending an air of leafy seclusion—a real treat for a Main Street inn!

There's plenty to do on Cape Cod, but one enjoyable recreation option is a small fleet of bicycles the Lloyds keep for guests.

MOSTLY HALL BED & BREAKFAST INN. 27 Main Street, Falmouth, MA 02540; (800) 682-0565, (508) 548-3786; Caroline and Jim Lloyd, owners. Open mid-Feb. through New Year's. Six corner rooms with queen beds, private baths, and air conditioning. Rates: $95 to $125 including full gourmet breakfast. Not suitable for children; no pets; no smoking; German spoken; all major credit cards. Complimentary bicycles. Summer and year-round theater.

DIRECTIONS: take Rte. 28 south to Falmouth to Main Street near village green.

CHARLES HINCKLEY HOUSE

Where no detail is overlooked

"A small, intimate country inn where great expectations are quietly met." The Charles Hinckley House's brochure tells the truth. The house defines elegant simplicity. Hosts Miya and Les Patrick are consummate professionals. Their goal is to indulge each guest with exquisite perfection.

Situated on the Olde Kings Highway in an historic district, the Federal Colonial house bespeaks warmth, relaxation, and romance. Every room boasts a working fireplace, private bath, and period furnishings that blend well with the rich plums and blues of the decor.

No details are overlooked. Miya's wildflower garden provides fresh bouquets to complement the exotic blooms she specially orders in. Her breakfast is a succulent testament to her aesthetic sense; choosing a combination of tropical and local fruits, she presents a platter so pleasing that it was featured in full color in *Country Living* magazine. Homemade *crème fraîche* is available

Hosts Miya and Les Patrick.

as an alternative to cream or milk, and handmade chocolates accompany the turn-down service. Flannel sheets in winter and cotton ones in summer dress the beds, with covers of down comforters or handcrafted quilts which add just the right amount of coziness. Guests also enjoy scented soaps, toiletries, thick-piled cotton bath sheets.

Evenings are casual, with impromptu gatherings in the living room; however, privacy is as easily achievable. Honeymooners can expect a bottle of champagne and breakfast in bed, if they wish.

Miya and Les, as young as they are, have been pampering people for years—first at The Inn at Phillips Mill in New Hope, Pennsylvania, then at Graywillow, also on the Cape—but never as well as they do now. A stay here will surely prove their expertise.

CHARLES HINCKLEY HOUSE. Box 723, Barnstable Village, MA 02630; (508) 362-9924, Fax (508) 362-8861; Les and Miya Patrick, innkeepers. Open year round. Rates: $119 to $149 with full breakfast. Four guest rooms, all with private baths and working fireplaces. Children over 12 welcome; no pets; no smoking; Visa/MasterCard/American Express.

DIRECTIONS: from Rte. 3 take Rte. 6 to exit 6. At the end of the ramp, turn left. Turn right onto 6A at the stop sign (½ mile down the road). Go 1½ miles more, and the house is on a slight rise.

Very special breakfasts.

ASHLEY MANOR

Celebrating the colonial period

The warmth and elegance of the colonial period are celebrated at Ashley Manor, a bed and breakfast inn nestled in the heart of Cape Cod's historic Barnstable village. The inn is a softly weathered Cape shingle that grew, over three centuries, to become a small estate surrounded by two park-like acres. The original section of the house traces its beginnings to 1699, built when Barnstable was a tiny fishing settlement. Wide, worn floorboards gleaming with the patina of age; a massive hearth complete with beehive ovens; and a secret passage, used during the Revolutionary War, reveal the age and character of the inn's first incarnation.

Today, innkeepers Donald and Fay Bain take pride in their gracious home, and they are careful to fill it with furnishings that conform to its rich colonial atmosphere. The Bains give equal atten-tion to providing life's graceful details, and to that end they fill rooms daily with fresh flowers; they offer guests an aperitif before dinner; and they stock bedside tables with a delightfully sinful cache of fine imported chocolates.

The inn contains six guest rooms, four of which are suites and five equipped with working fire-places. The floorboards in several of the rooms sport original "Nantucket spackle" paint, which has been carefully preserved, and each room is decorated with fine traditional fabrics, furnish-ings, wallcoverings, and antiques. The end result is thoroughly elegant and romantic.

Come the morning, guests find Donald hard at work in the kitchen preparing their morning feast. During summer months, breakfast at Ashley Manor is served *al fresco* on a brick terrace overlooking the inn's well-groomed grounds and new, private tennis court. When cool weather sets in, guests gather in the lovely old dining room. Here they relax in front of a blazing hearth and admire the Bains' collection of fine antique china.

ASHLEY MANOR. P.O. Box 856, 3660 Old Kings Highway (Rte. 6A), Barnstable, MA 02630; (508) 362-8044; Donald and Fay Bain, hosts. Open all year. Six rooms with private baths and air condi-tioning. Rates: $115 to $175, with full, multi course gourmet breakfast. Children over 14 welcome; no pets; Visa/MasterCard/ American Express; French spoken. Croquet and tennis on prem-ises; bicycles available. Swimming, tennis, golf, antiquing, arts and crafts, other Cape Cod activities.

DIRECTIONS: take Rte. 6A East through village of Barnstable to light. Go straight through light for 9/10 miles to manor on left.

The Olmsted Suite has two bedrooms and a sun deck.

Innkeepers Sal DiFlorio and Brian Gallo.

THE INN AT FERNBROOK

Gardens by Olmsted

This inn is a glorious reminder of what truly were "the good old days"—when summer homes were mansions, and gardens were replicas of Eden. In 1881, a Boston restaurateur built this sprawling Queen Anne Victorian and hired the famous landscape architect, Frederick Law Olmsted, to do the gardens on the surrounding seventeen acres. Olmsted, who designed New York's Central Park, created a magnificent retreat.

The inn itself is luxuriously decorated with Victorian furniture, but in a light, airy style. Rooms are flooded with sunshine through sheer curtains, and Oriental rugs complement softly-printed wallpapers in shades of cream-white. Each of the six guest rooms is very private, thanks to a design that has no two bedrooms sharing a common wall.

Honeymooners will particularly love staying in the Garden Cottage, a guest accommodation behind the main house, complete with the proverbial white picket fence. Also delightful is the third-floor suite.

A loft overlooks its living room, and it has its own sun deck with views of the gardens.

Though commercialism has claimed most of the Cape, guests will not feel its influence in Centerville, an 'un-touristy' town. Owners Brian Gallo and Sal DiFlorio have wonderful suggestions for visits to workshops of Cap Cod artisans. Brian can steer you to small shops and galleries offering everything from folk art to collectible glassware and colonial furniture. Sal is trained in European bodywork, and is available, by appointment, for relaxing therapeutic massage. Breakfast is four full courses, served in the dining room or on the porch.

You will be pleased to learn that, as a guest here, you are in good company. Those preceding you include Hollywood greats Cecil B. DeMille and Walt Disney, as well as Presidents Kennedy and Nixon!

THE INN AT FERNBROOK. 481 Main Street, Centerville, MA 02632; (508) 775-4334; Fax (508) 778-4455; Brian Gallo and Sal DiFlorio, owners. Open all year. Six guest rooms and a private one-room cottage, all with private baths; suite with private living room available. Rates: $125 to $185 double (less off season), including full, 4-course breakfast. Children over 13 welcome; no pets; smoking in parlor or on porch only; Italian spoken; all credit cards accepted. Wide range of dining nearby, including a Northern Italian, French country, and local seafood restaurant. All the usual Cape Cod activities.

DIRECTIONS: on the main street of Centerville, on Cape Cod off Rte. 6, exit 5.

An English country house ambience.

Wicker coolness on the porch.

WEDGEWOOD INN

An inn for all seasons

The affable hosts at the Wedgewood Inn, Milt and Gerrie Graham, came to innkeeping later in their lives, after eventful careers. Milt played professional football for the New England Patriots and the Ottawa Roughriders before becoming an FBI agent. Gerrie was both a professional dancer and school-teacher before being bitten by the bed and breakfast bug.

The area they settled on was the north side of Cape Cod, where they were attracted by the preserved maritime villages from colonial times. The particular inn they chose was in Yarmouth Port, and had opened as a bed and breakfast in 1983, after extensive refurbishing. It had been built in 1812 in the Federal style as the private home of an attorney.

The house is furnished with carefully selected antiques and period reproductions that create just the right ambience for a Federal home of the early 1800s. Handmade quilts, lace canopies, delightful nick-nacks, and Oriental rugs judiciously placed over the wide-planked pine floors complete the mood of those times.

Being open during the four seasons, woodburning fireplaces in four of the six guest rooms add their distinctive aroma to the atmosphere during crisp autumn and cold winter days.

The gardens are ablaze in spring, summer, and fall with plantings of annuals, perennials, and shrubs. Even in winter, a 200-year-old holly tree does its bit by imposing its brilliant red-colored berries on the landscape.

WEDGEWOOD INN, 83 Main Street (Rte. 6A), Yarmouth Port, MA 02675; (508) 362-5157; Milt and Gerrie Graham, innkeepers. Open all year. Six rooms with private baths, four with fireplaces. Rates: $115 to $160, including full breakfast of pancakes, waffles, French toast, bacon, sausage, fruit, and coffee; (off-season rates available). Children over 10 welcome, no pets; limited smoking; Visa/MasterCard/American Express/Diners Club. Restaurants and shops within walking distance.

DIRECTIONS: from Rte. 6 (Mid-Cape Hwy) take exit 6 (Willow St.) right onto Willow to Rte. 6A. Turn right on 6A and inn will be on the right.

THE OVER LOOK INN

A haven of British hospitality

When sea captain Barnabas Chipman built his home in 1869, he sited it on the outer reaches of Cape Cod, close enough to the Atlantic Ocean to feel a part of the sea. More than a century later, Chipman's three-story Victorian clapboard home is a bed and breakfast inn and, sitting at the edge of the Cape Cod National Seashore and close to the Audubon Wildlife Sanctuary, it offers overnight guests proximity both to the sea and to the Cape's wild but delicate natural beauty.

Besides its great location, the Over Look Inn is a haven of traditional British hospitality personified by Scottish-born innkeepers Nan and Ian Aitchison, and their sons Mark and Clive. The Aitchisons painstakingly restored this vintage sea captain's home to a gleaming finish, painting it soft butter yellow. They also diligently groom the inn's spacious lawn, which is wooded with mature

A brand new guest room.

shade trees that completely seclude it from neighbors.

The spirit of the British Isles is felt in the library, which is furnished with a leather couch and a working fireplace, because it is filled with books and memorabilia relating to Winston Churchill. And just down the hall, the Victorian billiards room seems a mandatory accoutrement to a proper British great house.

Continuing the tradition of their native island, the Aitchisons serve a full English breakfast each morning, often featuring the Scottish specialty *kedgeree*, a savory mixture of finnan haddie, rice, onions, chopped eggs, and raisins, sautéed in butter and served with a generous helping of mango chutney. At tea-time guests are supplied with traditional scones, hot and flaky and straight from the oven.

THE OVER LOOK INN. Rte. 6 (County Road), Eastham, Cape Cod, MA 02642; (508) 255-1886, Fax (508) 240-0345, (800) 356-1121. Ian and Nan Aitchison, hosts, with son Mark. Open all year. Eleven rooms with private baths in main house; 3 suites in renovated 18th-century barn. Rates: $80 to $100 double, with full English breakfast and afternoon tea. Children welcome; no pets; smoking in library; all major credit cards. Billiards, croquet, bicycles, swimming, tennis, golf. Excellent dining nearby.

DIRECTIONS: 3 miles beyond Orleans rotary, across from Salt Pond Visitor Center of Cape Cod.

The Billiard Room in the new section.

DAVE MONAGHAN PHOTOGRAPHS

CLIFF LODGE

Sample the romance of island living

Once the province of whaling barons, who built stately mansions on cobblestone streets, Nantucket is now an elite summer retreat of cedar-shake beach houses, gourmet restaurants, boutiques, and bed and breakfasts: To sample the old days there is the Nantucket Whaling Museum, where the island's history is celebrated.

Pretty enough to have graced the cover of *Country Home* magazine, Cliff Lodge belies its 1771 birth-date. Previously run as Harbor House, and just five minutes from the center of town, it was given a facelift by two women from Nantucket Island Antiques. Using soft blues and whites, Laura Ashley wallpapers and fabrics, and framed pastoral prints, they created a light cheerful feeling in the eleven guest rooms, six of which have ocean views. Sprightly in décor, the entire house is furnished with bright wicker, antique pine pieces, and spatter-painted floors.

A second-floor alcove, with its wicker chairs and writing table, is perfect for relaxation, as is the second-floor porch that overlooks the harbor and Jetty's Beach. For those who dote on a panoramic

view, there are steps leading up to the widow's walk, where the view spans the entire island.

Breakfast includes delicious homemade muffins or fruit breads which can be eaten in front of the fireplace in the breakfast room.

In 1990, the national newspaper *USA Today* included Cliff Lodge as one of the ten most romantic inns in the country. Need we say more?

CLIFF LODGE. 9 Cliff Road, Nantucket, MA 02554; (508) 228-9480, Fax (508) 228-6308; Debby and John Bennett, owner/innkeepers. Open all year. Eleven rooms and full apartment with private entrance, all with private baths, TVs, telephones. Rates: $65 to $85 single, $85 to $165 double, $135 to $225 for apartment, varying with seasons. Includes ample continental breakfast plus afternoon tea in season. Children 12 and over welcome; no pets; no smoking; Visa/MasterCard. Parking on premises.

DIRECTIONS: 10 minutes from ferry, 5 minutes from downtown.

The Capt. Harding Room has a fireplace and a bay window.

CAPTAIN DEXTER HOUSE

Island living at its best

Three blocks from the ferry, and the first home in the historic residential district of Vineyard Haven, The Captain Dexter House stands as a model of elegance, comfort, and convenience. Guests here can experience island living at its best—without billboards, fast-food franchises, not even stoplights—only picturesque seaside villages, quiet harbors, and glorious white sand beaches.

Martha's Vineyard is world-renowned for its natural beauty as well as its celebrities. The flat, straight southern shore provides miles of glacially carved, wave-dashed beach. The gentle curves on the island's other two sides lead into the calmer waters of Nantucket Sound to the east and Vineyard Sound to the west. North and center lies the year-round town.

The innkeeper likes to describe the old sea captain's house as a "Federalized Victorian" with a peaked roof, bay windows, and side porch, but the interior recalls colonial times. A Williamsburg-style reproduction table assumes center stage in the dining room, flanked by Queen Anne-style chairs and beyond by a Sheraton breakfront and a Scottish grandfather clock that dates back to 1812. The far wall hosts two portraits painted in 1843, the same year that the house was built.

The eight well-kept guest rooms reflect the consideration put into the common rooms. Antiques and contemporary furnishings provide a pleasing mix that suits modern demands for comfort and charm.

THE CAPTAIN DEXTER HOUSE, Box 2457, 100 Main Street, Vineyard Haven, Martha's Vineyard, MA 02568; (508) 693-6564, Fax (508) 693-8448; Roberta Pieczenik, owner. Open all year. Eight guest rooms, all with private baths, two with working fireplaces. Rates: $115 to $165 in season; $85 to $145 off-season; $20 for an additional person. Children over 12 welcome; no pets; smoking in garden only; MasterCard/Visa/American Express. Continental breakfast. Guest refrigerator, beach towels, garage for bicycles. Watersports; horseback riding; summer theater; good restaurants nearby.

DIRECTIONS: Car reservations to and from Woods Hole should be made well in advance. Write or call the Parkers.

RHODE ISLAND

ADMIRAL FITZROY INN

An inn to lift your spirits

An immaculate three-story, weathered-shingle hotel, the Admiral Fitzroy, one of the most enjoyable inns in Newport, is the brainchild of owner Jane Berriman and her husband Bruce. It is just one of three sister inns—the others being the Admiral Benbow and the Admiral Farragut—operated by the Berrimans, and each has its own character and style. The Berrimans are seasoned travelers who bring to innkeeping a refined sense of what the road-weary relish. At the Admiral Fitzroy this means all the amenities of an intimate, fine hotel with an abundance of grace notes usually reserved for home-style bed and breakfast inns.

The Admiral Fitzroy is tucked well away from the busy thoroughfare of Thames Street, but it offers wonderful views of the harbor and is perfectly located for walking the town. The inn is artfully conceived and is a showcase for fine craftsmanship, from the hand-carved Admiral Fitzroy plaque in the lobby (which was created by Bruce, a master woodcarver) to the hand painted, lacquered, and glazed wall treatments that add luster and richness to each room. Beds are dressed in fine linens, topped by plush down comforters. The innkeepers also attend to such welcome details as using fresh herbs in the breakfast omelet and offering guests fresh mint to flavor their coffee and tea.

The quality of service at the Admiral Fitzroy is top-notch. The inn's fine staff is congenial and one and all take great pride in working for this special inn.

ADMIRAL FITZROY INN. 398 Thames Street, Newport, RI 02840; (800) 343-2863, (401) 846-4256, Fax (401) 848-8006; Jane Berriman, proprietor; Holly Eastman, host. Open all year. Eighteen rooms with private baths. Rates: winter $85 to $150; summer $125 to $200, with full breakfast. Children welcome; no pets; all major credit cards. Newport activities, including sailing, swimming, golf. Extensive dining opportunities.

DIRECTIONS: located in downtown Newport, on the main street facing the harbor.

A top-floor bedroom, with balcony, overlooks Newport harbor.

Pampered luxury typical of Newport living.

FRANCIS MALBONE HOUSE

A shipping merchant's mansion

Attributed to Peter Harrison, architect of the Touro Synagogue and the Redwood Library, this historic inn was built in 1760 for Colonel Francis Malbone. Having made his fortune as a shipping merchant, Malbone moored his fleet in Newport Harbor across from his mansion. Legend has it that there was once an underground tunnel from the waterfront to the mansion through which the colonel smuggled goods to avoid paying duty to King George.

Painstakingly maintained throughout the years, and a private residence until 1989, the mansion has eight guest rooms and one suite. Furnished in the Queen Anne style, with wide floor boards and four poster beds, some of the rooms have working fireplaces, and each is painted in either terra cotta, Dresden blue, hunter green, or burgundy.

Two sitting rooms on the first floor face the harbor, one room still paneled in the original 1760 carved wood. Both have inside shutters. A third sitting room houses the library.

Breakfast is served in the dining room, originally the mansion's kitchen, with its open walk-in hearth. Peach crêpes, eggs Benedict, and strawberry Belgian waffles are favorite offerings.

A large terrace in the walled-in garden is perfect for dining outdoors, where a flowering dogwood tree towers over the fountain. A paper bark maple, a copper beech, dahlias, and rhododendron all add to the lovely, serene ambience of this colonial mansion in the heart of the waterfront district.

THE FRANCIS MALBONE HOUSE. 392 Thames Street, Newport, RI 02840; (800) 846-0392, (401) 846-0392, Fax (401) 848-5956; Will Dewey, innkeeper. Open all year. Eight guest rooms and 1 suite, all with private baths. Rates: $160 to $295 in season (May 1 to Oct. 31); $125 to $195 off season (all rates per room). Includes full gourmet breakfast. Children over 12 welcome; no pets; no smoking; Visa/MasterCard/American Express. Recommended restaurants include The Place, White Horse Tavern, Scales and Shells, The Black Pearl. The fabulous attractions of Newport include the Tennis Hall of Fame, Touro Synagogue, Redwood Library, music festivals, world-class tennis, and yachting.

DIRECTIONS: located downtown on the harborfront. For guest parking take third left off Thames onto Brewer St.

Owners Priscilla and Thomas Malone.

Details in the Windsor Suite.

ELM TREE COTTAGE

The Gilded Age of Newport

Arrive at the door to this breathtaking bed and breakfast and you return to the gilded age of Newport. Guests are delighted to be part of the casual ritziness that has been perfectly recreated by Thomas and Priscilla Malone. It comes as no surprise that both were trained as professional artists, since the ambience and décor reveal a special touch and attention to detail.

Priscilla moves furniture around with the seasons—to face the magnificent seaward twenty-five-foot bay windows in the summer and to cozy seating arrangements by the fireside in chilly weather. The floral prints, textures, and colors everywhere are harmonious and artful. Thomas' work as a master stained-glass artist is seen throughout the inn.

The six guest accommodations are spectacular, decorated with fine antiques from England and

Left above, the Windsor suite is truly royal. Below, the Library Bedroom.

France, as well as Newport estate pieces. All of the beds are carved Louis XV queens and kings covered with opulent arrays of linens and pillows. Priscilla does a special turndown each night, bidding guests sweet dreams with treats on a doily. The Windsor Suite, named for onetime Elm Tree Cottage guest, Wallace Simpson, Duchess of Windsor, is luxury personified. At one-thousand square feet, it includes a king-sized bed, a chandeliered boudoir, two living room arrangements, and a working fireplace.

Breakfast is served at private tables in the dining room. Favorite entrées include French apple crêpes in raspberry sauce in the shape of a calla lilly, a mango melon tart with cream cheese, or eggs Benedict with orange sauce on corned beef hash.

ELM TREE COTTAGE, 336 Gibbs Avenue, Newport, RI 02840; (800) 882-3356, (401) 849-1610; Thomas and Priscilla Malone, owners. Open all year except January. Five large guest rooms and one suite, all with private baths, air conditioning, and king or queen beds; most with working fireplaces. Rates: summer $175 to $325, winter $135 to $295 (per room—max. of 2 guests), including full gourmet breakfast. Children over 14 welcome in own room; no pets; no smoking; Visa/MasterCard/American Express. Excellent dining within walking distance. 1½ blocks to ocean beach and the famous Cliff Walk. Music festivals in summer and Christmas in Newport festival in winter.

DIRECTIONS: given upon reservation.

MARSHALL SLOCUM HOUSE

Lobster al fresco

Here is a classic bed and breakfast with the quintessential motherly innkeeper, Joan Wilson, who offers warmth and style in a convivial setting on a street of residential Victorians in the center of Newport. Having raised a family and run an orange grove, she now does innkeeping with flair. "It's a stage, and I get to play at what I do," says Joan.

What she does is provide six guest rooms, charmingly decorated, and a wonderful sit-down breakfast under a chandelier in the dining room. Joan changes the table linens, plates and color scheme daily—as well as the menu. One day may bring a plum tablecloth, yellow cloth napkins, and Portuguese majolica platters of Belgian waffles with fresh strawberries. The following morning the same table will be laid with traditional blue-and-white china on which guests are treated to hash. Says Joan: "Hash sounds like an ugly word, but *my* hash is to die for!"

The inn is decorated in "eclectic Joan Wilson," which is perfect for a Newport Victorian, with its many special touches. There are plenty of nautical prints in keeping with local history. Bedrooms are cheery. A bright yellow room on the second floor has a springtime feeling, with a hand-painted bureau that matches the trellised rose pattern on the bedspreads. Other rooms offer patchwork quilts and canopies, or white wicker furnishings.

The Slocum House is a great choice for groups or couples traveling together. Joan loved European pensions she stayed at on her travels, and models her place on that style of hospitality. In fact, she has repeat guests that met at her inn and now plan yearly reunions there. In keeping with this is a Joan Wilson special—Wednesday night lobster dinner. Any guests staying for three nights that include Wednesday are treated to a traditional lobster dinner served al fresco on the back deck, checkered tablecloth, bibs, and all.

Left above, the Marshall Slocum House is big on lobster, the ultimate New England treat. Below, a guest room.

Owner Joan Wilson.

1855 MARSHALL SLOCUM HOUSE. 29 Kay Street, Newport, RI 02840; (800) 372-5120, (401) 841-5120; Joan Wilson, owner. Open all year. Six guest rooms, some with private baths, some sharing; 2 rooms can sleep 3. Rates: summer $70 to $100, winter $60 to $80, including full sit-down breakfast with different menu and table setting each day. Children over 12 welcome; no pets; no smoking; Visa/MasterCard/American Express. Casual to elegant dining within walking distance. (Joan will serve dinner, provide picnic meals, or cater dinner parties by arrangement.) Mansion tours, beaches, sailing, antiquing, shopping, and galleries in Newport are a treat.

DIRECTIONS: map and directions sent upon receipt of reservations.

The breakfast table.

WAYSIDE GUEST HOUSE

On the Street of Dreams

This 1896 Newport "Summer Cottage" is across from The Elms and down the block from Belcourt Castle, Mrs. Astor's Beechwood, and the venerable Rosecliff, where *The Great Gatsby* was filmed.

Everything in the interior is generously proportioned with fifteen-foot ceilings on the parlor floor, and twelve-foot ceilings in the guest rooms. The nine bedchambers are elegantly ample, and each has a large sitting area where breakfast may be enjoyed in the privacy of the room. All of the rooms are furnished with turn-of-the-century furniture, and five of the rooms have beautifully detailed decorative fireplaces. All have private baths.

Outdoors there is a heated in-ground swimming pool, provided with deck chairs and chaises, and surrounded by poplars and beech trees. A barbecue and picnic tables are available for those who choose to eat on the grounds.

Great restaurants are easy to find, and the Posts recommend White Horse Tavern, The Black Pearl, and La Petite Auberge for formal dining. Try The Canfield House or The Moorings for casual fare.

Dorothy Post dreamed of having a bed and breakfast when she was in high school and wrote of it in her senior yearbook. In 1976 she and her husband Al bought the Wayside, which once served as a girls' dorm for Newport College. After fifteen years of owning and managing the Wayside with their son Don and daughter-in-law Debbie, Dorothy is glad her day dream came true.

WAYSIDE GUEST HOUSE. 406 Bellevue Avenue, Newport, RI 02840; (800) 653-7678, (401) 847-0302, Fax (401) 848-9374; Dorothy, Al, and Don Post, owners and managers. Open all year. Nine guest rooms with private baths. Rates: in season $115 to $150; off season $75 to $105, double, including continental breakfast. Children welcome; no pets; smoking allowed; no credit cards. Heated pool on premises.

DIRECTIONS: on Bellevue Ave. across the street from The Elms.

Lifestyle in the Grand Manner.

CLIFFSIDE INN

The luxury of the Victorian age

Cliffside Inn capturs the grandeur of the Victorian age with flowing curtains, bay windows, and commodious common rooms. This Second Empire summer cottage, which now stands among many beautiful houses in a peaceful residential district, once dominated the acreage.

The thirteen guest rooms, all with private bath facilities, are imaginatively decorated. The coral and dark sea green of Miss Adele's Room is incorporated into a fireplace mantel that now functions as a headboard for the queen-sized bed. The Miss Beatrice Room, a favorite with newlyweds, is dressed in pinks and blues with bay windows and a Lincoln bed. The newest accommodation is the Tower Suite, a two-level guest chamber in a twenty-five-foot tower. Recently redecorated is the Seascape Suite, now bathed in rose and pastel greens, with a skylight over the bed.

Cliffside has an unusual history. Built in 1880, the house served as a summer retreat for the governor of Maryland. Sixteen years later it became the site of a private preparatory school. The most famous denizen was Beatrice Pastorius Turner, who gained fame as a self-portrait artist and who painted the mother-daughter oil painting that hangs in the living room on the wall to the right of the piano. Her notoriety, however, came from her eccentricities. A recluse obsessed with youth, she walked into the town wearing Victorian clothes up until the 1940s.

Cliff Walk is about a ten-minute stroll away; the beach, even closer. All in all, Cliffside is a welcome addition to Newport's attractions.

CLIFFSIDE INN. 2 Seaview Avenue, Newport, RI 02840; (800) 845-1811, (401) 847-1811, Fax (401) 848-5850; Stephan Nicolas, innkeeper. Open all year. Thirteen guest rooms, all with private baths, air conditioning, Cable TV, phones; 10 with working fireplaces, 2 with whirlpool 2-person tubs. Rates: $145 to $325. The rate includes tax and a full breakfast and evening hors d'oeuvres. Children over 13 welcome; no pets; no smoking; all major credit cards.

DIRECTIONS: from I-95, take Rte. 138 over the Newport Bridge. Take a right onto Americas Cup Ave. and bear left onto Memorial Blvd. Take a right onto Cliff Ave. The inn is on the left, at the corner of Sea View Ave.

The Moon Mist Room.

The breakfast room.

THE RICHARDS

A gracious country mansion

Past a "dead-end" sign where a sandy road meets the woods, is this gracious country mansion. Walking by the lush perennial flower gardens bordering the drive, the distant *ponk* of a tennis ball is heard. The air is a mixture of sea and forest breezes. You know you've found a perfect getaway.

The inn was built of Narragansett pier granite in 1884 by an eccentric who had admired stone country manors in England. Now it's home to Nancy and Steven Richards as well as a marvelous bed and breakfast for the guests they welcome.

The down-to-earth hosts have found the right balance between elegance and a country atmosphere. Of her amazing home Nancy says, "This is *really* our home and this is *really* us." Ardent antiquers, the couple has chosen terrific pieces for the many rooms and, says Nancy, *all* the furnishings have stories. She has a wonderful flair for textiles and sophisticated colors, from coral-dominated Oriental

Left, owners Steven and Nancy Richards.

rugs in the main hall to shades of celandine and hydrangea in the guest rooms. Nancy is particularly interested in historic fabrics. The décor is constantly evolving, much to the delight of repeat visitors.

Every bedroom has a sitting area and a working fireplace. The Yellow Room is cheery, with a French country feeling and an ecru lace canopy on the bed. The Moon Mist Room has beautiful antique twin sleigh beds that came with the house. There is also a very large and private suite that's perfect for two couples vacationing together. Off its own hallway, it has two bedrooms, a sitting room, and a bath.

Breakfast is a full meal served family style under a chandelier. The menu is mouthwatering, with fruits, homemade breads and muffins, and entrées that include soufflés, blintzes, or a recent new recipe, kahlua mocha pancakes with hot orange sauce.

THE RICHARDS. 144 Gibson Avenue, Narragansett, RI 02882-3937; (401) 789-7746; Nancy and Steven Richards, owners. Open all year. Four large guest rooms and one suite with 2 bedrooms, all with sitting areas and private baths except one sharing. Rates: $65 to $125 per room, including full breakfast served family style; 4-night minimum during August. Children 12 and over welcome; no pets; no smoking; no credit cards. Many restaurants in area, from clam shacks to French and Spanish cuisine. Foxwoods Casino, Mystic Seaport, summer theater, Block Island ferry nearby. Great antiquing in area.

DIRECTIONS: 1½ hours from Boston, 40 minutes from Providence; call for specifics.

THE SASAFRASH

A cornucopia of antiques

Here's where you learn *never* to judge an inn by its cover! Coming upon the shingled simplicity of this former primitive Methodist Church, built in 1907, you expect a similarly humble interior. Step inside and you're amazed.

If you've ever fantasized about spending the night in a truly beautiful antique shop, this may be the place. Except that it is not an antique shop anymore. Owners Shirley and Sanford Kessler used the building as a summer antique store for years. They specialized in island estate furnishings and paintings, their shop becoming somewhat of a social center on Block Island. Heading for retirement, they renovated THE SASAFRASH to be their year-round home. People urged them to try it as a bed and breakfast. They did, and have been enjoying the innkeeping life ever since.

Guests make themselves at home all over the first-floor tri-level salon, spreading out at the many richly furnished seating areas or setting up a card game at the handkerchief table in a corner.

The lovely guest rooms are upstairs in the former choir loft. Décor is simple Victorian, with antique beds and leaded glass windows. Each is named after a former pastor of the church.

At breakfast guests enjoy a full meal, with a hot dish that may include baked poached eggs, waffles or an egg strata. Guests often end the meal by wandering out to the breezy back deck with a cup of coffee and a slice of homebaked breakfast cake. There they contemplate a day of beaches, nature, salt air, relaxation, maybe some fishing or a bike ride, ending with a dinner of marvelous fresh Block Island swordfish.

The stained-glass windows have been retained.

THE SASAFRASH. P.O. Box 1227, Block Island, RI 02807; (on Center Road); (401) 466-5486; Shirley and Sanford Kessler, owners. Open May through October. Four guest rooms, 2 with private baths, 2 sharing. Rates: $85 to $120 (2 night minimum, 3 nights on holiday weekends), including full breakfast in dining room. Young teens accepted; no pets; no smoking; no credit cards. Great restaurants on Island, casual attire everywhere. Great beaches, fishing, bike riding, sailing, kayaking, surfing, bird watching, nature trails; 2 movie theaters on this 7 by 13 mile island.

DIRECTIONS: Ferry from New London, CT, Pt. Judith, RI, or Montauk, NY. Kesslers will pick up at Old Harbor 1 mile away. Cars not necessary, but ferry reservations for them are necessary far in advance.

Left above, the old church exudes the charm of weathered shingles. Below, the richly furnished first-floor salon, stuffed with antiques.

A guest room.

The inn portico.

Breakfast at the pool.

THE VILLA

A Mediterranean flavor

Imagine finding a Mediterranean getaway minutes from the beach in Rhode Island! That's what visitors discover at The Villa, a 1930s-era stucco cottage that's been reincarnated from the Italian coast. Brilliant flowers line the drive up to the inn's centerpiece, a huge Mediterranean tiled pool and fountain surrounded by gardens and terraces.

A carriage house at one end of the pool accommodates two of the inn's most alluring guest quarters. Upstairs is La Sala di Verona, also known as the Romeo and Juliet Suite. It is a spacious, romantic retreat, with a cathedral ceiling and skylights above a king-sized brass bed, a living room and dining area, a Jacuzzi, and of course, a private balcony. Downstairs is The Blue Grotto, a cozy room with wicker furniture and a natural stone wall.

Left above, the pool area, where the living is easy.
Below, the Rosa Maiorano Room.

The remaining guest accommodations, mostly suites, are in the main house. All are tastefully furnished in traditional style and rich colors. For example, the third-floor Cielo Room is the size of an apartment and includes a kitchenette and living room with pull-out sofa.

Owner Jerry Maiorano is a caring and attentive host, who oversees all the details of this inn. Over half of his guests are celebrating a special occasion. If he knows about it, Jerry will provide a card, chocolates, a balloon, champagne, or whatever is appropriate. The Villa is an ideal place to hold a wedding, small party, or reunion. There is a large lawn next to the pool area that is perfect for a lawn tent.

THE VILLA, 190 Shore Road, Westerly, RI 02891; (401) 596-1054; Jerry Maiorano, owner. Open all year. Six suites and one guest room, all with private baths, air conditioning, cable TV, and refrigerators; 3 with Jacuzzis. Rates: $95 to $195 in season, $65 to $175 off season, including buffet breakfast in season and hot breakfast in cooler weather. Well-behaved children accepted; pets welcome in the 3 rooms with private entrances; smoking allowed; Italian spoken; Visa/MasterCard/American Express. Nearby dining includes oceanfront seafood 2 minutes away. Golf next door, tennis nearby, ocean beaches 5 minutes, Watch Hill 10 minutes, Mystic Seaport, Foxwoods 20 minutes.

DIRECTIONS: from New York City take I-95 north to exit 92 onto Rte. 2 east to Rte. 78 toward beaches. On 78 cross Rte. 1 and take left at first stop sign; continue to light and take left on Shore Road (scenic 1A north). Villa is one mile on left after golf course.

CONNECTICUT

The Emily Dickinson Room.

THE OLD MYSTIC INN

Built during the heyday of whaling

This picturesque country colonial is tucked away in the quiet hamlet of Old Mystic, just minutes north of the more well-known village of Mystic. Visitors flock there to the Seaport Museum, aquarium, craft galleries, and charter sailing trips. But all is peaceful at the red inn with its huge maple trees, gazebo and white picket fence. In fact, this bed and breakfast and the country store across the street, both owned by Mary and Peter Knight, pretty much make up the "downtown" of Old Mystic!

The inn was built in 1794, during the area's heyday as a center for whaling and ship building. More recently it was a well-known bookstore.

After the Knights reclaimed the first floor of the inn from the 20,000 books that had been shelved there, they chose to name each of the eight guest rooms for New England authors. The accommodations are welcoming and thoughtfully presented. Each has a synopsis of the life of the author it honors along with his or her works to enjoy. And each is unique, with hand stenciling, antiques, patchwork quilts, or comforters in delightful colors.

The Old Mystic Inn is a great place to relax at any time of the year. There's a remarkable fireplace

Left, the inn literally invites you in.

Owners Peter and Mary Knight.

in the keeping room, roaring in the chilly months. The yard offers stunning leaves in the fall and shady areas by the stone walls for lounging on lazy summer days. The area is popular with cyclists. Local bike trails are five-to-fifty miles long through bucolic countryside.

THE OLD MYSTIC INN. P.O. Box 634, Old Mystic, CT 06372-0634/ (52 Main Street); (860) 572-9422; Mary and Peter Knight, owners. Open all year. Seven rooms and one suite, all with private baths and air conditioning and some with whirlpool tubs or fireplaces. Rates: $115 to $135 April to Nov. with 2-night minimum, $95 to $125 in winter; includes full country breakfast at separate tables in dining room. Children welcome (rollaways available); no pets; no smoking in rooms; Visa/MasterCard/American Express. Recommend JP Daniels for fine dining in restored barn. Huge choice of activities nearby—Mystic Seaport, aquarium, Foxwoods, USS Nautilus, summer theater at Eugene O'Neill Center, Westerly Playhouse, Goodspeed Opera House.

DIRECTIONS: from south on I-95 take exit 90 onto Rte. 27 north to stop sign in center of Old Mystic by country store. Turn right to inn on right.

The Russell Room.

APPLEWOOD FARMS INN

Yankee hospitality on 33 acres

If you've ever wished you had an old Yankee farm in the country to go home to for a vacation, Applewood Farms is the place for you. Authentically antique, from its wide-planked floors to the well-chosen furnishings, this center-chimney colonial offers country relaxation without any country affectations.

Innkeepers Frankie and Tom Betz purchased the farm in 1985 and renovated it from the sills and joists up. Built in 1826, the home is now an inviting and comfortable bed and breakfast on thirty-three acres. There are sheep for local color and a horse named Pat. All year round there is peace and quiet.

Furnishings are eclectic and wonderful. Before the Betzes opened the inn, Frankie went shopping for antiques for three months solid and put together a varied collection.

The parlor is Victorian and the dining room colonial, with a woodburning stove glowing in chilly weather. The Russell Room on the first floor has a marvelous Victorian bedroom set, including a curlicue-carved vanity with fan-shaped mirror, red print wallpaper and a lace bedspread. The Ben Adams Room upstairs has a more spare colonial décor, with lots of white, a king-sized antique bed and a view of the gazebo. Four rooms have working fireplaces, which Tom will gladly lay for you.

But it's the extra touches that count. There are baskets of magazines and a reproduction antique radio at every bedside. Small collectibles and antique paintings are displayed throughout the house. And everywhere are groupings of quaint black and white photos, some of the Betz family.

APPLEWOOD FARMS INN. 528 Colonel Ledyard Highway, Ledyard, CT 06339; (860) 536-2022; Frankie and Tom Betz, owners. Open all year. Four guest rooms and one 2-bedroom suite, all with private baths and air conditioning. Most have fireplaces. Rates: $115 to $250 per room ($25 for third person), including full family-style breakfast. Children welcome by prior arrangement; pets welcome; no smoking in bedrooms; Visa/MasterCard/American Express. Favorite dining recommended 5 minutes away includes Italian in an old tavern and American in a restored barn. Ten minutes to Mystic Seaport, aquarium, shops, and sailing. Foxwoods Casino 6 miles.

DIRECTIONS: from south on I-95 take exit 89 north onto Cow Hill Road. At 2nd light turn left on Rte. 184 (Gold Star Hwy) and at next light turn right on Colonel Ledyard Hwy and go 2½ miles to inn on right.

Pat, a resident of the farm.

Left above, a charming detail of the bureau and a corner of the parlor. Below, the Russell Room.

The Artist's Room.

THE QUEEN ANNE INN

Distinctively decorated rooms

In this classic Queen Anne 1903 Victorian there are three floors of restored and delightfully decorated rooms. The view out front may be a busy street on the edge of this former whaling city, but the inn is an island of turn-of-the-century living.

The ambience starts with tea and sweets in the parlor every afternoon, a nice welcome for arriving guests. There are wonderful collections of antique tea sets throughout the first floor, in celebration of the teatime tradition.

Eight guest rooms are all distinct, with eclectic furnishings and wallpapers that add a wonderful authenticity to the décor. Accommodations range from the distinguished first-floor Captain's Room, with original wood paneling, brass bed, and working fireplace, to the lofty and extremely spacious Tower Suite on the third floor. There guests enjoy a full kitchen in the turret as well as a living room area. It is a great choice for those planning a long stay

Left above, a perfect example of a Queen Anne house. Below, the Bridal Room.

and is popular with business travelers who can hold meetings there.

Innkeepers Janet and Ed serve a sit-down breakfast at small tables set around the periphery of the front parlor. Janet hosts while Ed is in the kitchen preparing his lemon soufflé pancakes and apple cinnamon stuffed French toast. He is also the genius behind the baked goods at tea time, including tasty sweet/tart lemon tea bars and gingerbreads.

The Queen Anne is conveniently located for travelers. The Coast Guard Academy and Connecticut College are just up the road. Mystic is fifteen minutes away, and so is the Foxwoods Casino. Nearby Ocean Beach State Park has an old-fashioned boardwalk, with musical performances and festivals, including an annual polka celebration.

THE QUEEN ANNE INN, 265 Williams Street, New London, CT 06320; (800) 347-8818, (860) 447-2600; Janet Yarbrough-Moody and Ed Boncich, innkeepers. Open all year. Ten guest rooms, 8 with private baths and 2 sharing; all with air conditioning, some with phones and TVs. Rates: $89 to $185 per room; singles $5 less, extra person $25; includes full sit-down gourmet breakfast. Children 12 and over accepted; no pets; no smoking; Visa/MasterCard/American Express/Discover. Seafood and other dining nearby, bistros within walking distance. New London central to Mystic, Foxwoods, ferries to Block Island and Fishers Island, Eugene O'Neill Theater Center, USS Nautilus.

DIRECTIONS: from I-95 northbound take exit 83 and turn right at end of ramp to inn ¼ mile on left.

Built in 1820.

Owners Tom and Ann Gray.

ANTIQUES & ACCOMMODATIONS

Antiques to go

Elegance, sophistication, gracious country living, and a house full of fine furnishings, virtually all for sale, is what happens when two antiques dealers marry and open an inn. Located in the quiet village of North Stonington, Ann and Tom Gray offer warm hospitality in luxurious surroundings. Says Ann, "The inn is formal, but we're informal."

The Grays have two buildings for guests, both meticulously decorated. The main house is a charming yellow Victorian with a mix of formal English and American antiques. The 1820 House is behind, across the English-style cottage gardens, and is done up in early American with country antiques.

All guests feast daily on a four-course candlelight breakfast. Tom does most of the cooking and admits that "I'm a Napoleon in the kitchen," and his cooking is certainly worthy of emperors. The menu may include a compote of pears in raspberry sauce with orange liqueur, homemade breads, chilled cantaloupe soup, salmon aquavit omelettes, or perhaps a version of eggs Benedict made with crab.

The main house has three lovely guest rooms, one a two-room suite. Susan's Room is popular with honeymooners, with its delicate floral wallpaper and a four-poster canopied bed. A curving central staircase affords a wavy view of the other house through original glass in the stairwell window.

Downstairs in the 1820 House is an unusual find for a bed and breakfast—the Family Suite. It has its own spacious and cheerful country kitchen (fully equipped) and three bedrooms, one with fireplace and exposed beams. The entryway is private, and the suite is a wonderful choice for longer stays. One

Left above, an elegant setting for a silver service. Below, Jeni's Room.

memorable guest was dropped off by a chauffeur and stayed for a month.

ANTIQUES AND ACCOMMODATIONS. 32 Main Street, North Stonington, CT 06359; (800) 554-7829, (860) 535-1736; Ann and Tom Gray, owners. Open all year. Two guest rooms and one suite in main house and two guest rooms and one 3-bedroom suite in 1820 House in back, all with private baths and air conditioning; some have fireplaces. Rates: $99 to $229 depending on season, including 4-course candlelight breakfast and afternoon refreshments. Children who appreciate antiques welcome; no pets; no smoking; German spoken; Visa/MasterCard. Water Street Cafe in Stonington recommended for gourmet dining. Foxwoods 5 minutes, Mystic 15 minutes, Watch Hill village and beaches 20 minutes.

DIRECTIONS: from I-95 going north take exit 92 to Rte. 2 west. Go 2.2 miles past shops to sign for North Stonington and turn right to inn at corner on right.

The formal living room.

RED BROOK INN

A colonial gem near Mystic Seaport

Sitting in a California Victorian house filled with a lifetime's collection of Early American antiques, Ruth Keyes came to the conclusion that she would never feel altogether at home in the West. An old fashioned girl at heart, she dreamt of Connecticut and a colonial village like Old Mystic. Within six months of her return to the East, she owned the beautiful 1770 Creary Homestead.

A recent and welcome addition expanding the inn is The Historic Haley Tavern, originally a stage coach stop. Restored and beautifully appointed, its rooms include The Ross Haley Chamber with antique furnishings and working fireplace, The Mary Virginia Chamber, a beautiful Early American room with a canopied queen bed, and The Victorian Nancy Creary Chamber with its own whirlpool tub.

Under Ruth's guardianship, the Red Brook Inn is a colonial showcase; her collection of furniture and artifacts perfectly complements both the lines and the spirit of the house. All of the rooms are filled with period antiques, from the second-floor bedrooms with their blanket chests and early lighting devices, to the first-floor keeping room with its original cooking fireplace, beehive oven, and iron crane and cookware. Each four-poster or canopied bed is coordinated with carefully chosen matching quilts and linens.

A full breakfast, served on the long harvest table in the keeping room, might include quiche, baked or fresh fruit, walnut waffles, baked eggs, or pumpkin pancakes with sausage.

THE RED BROOK INN. Box 237, Rte. 184 at Wells Rd., Old Mystic, CT 06372; (800) 290-5619, (860) 572-0349, Ruth Keyes, proprietor; Tom Murphy, innkeeper. Colonial gem built around 1770. Historic Haley Tavern circa 1740. Open year-round. Eleven guest rooms; all with private baths, eight with working fireplaces. Rates: $95 to $189 per double room, including full breakfast. Inquire about Saturday night winter-time open hearth dinners and a fabulous weekend package. No pets; no smoking in building; Visa/MasterCard. Mystic Seaport Museum, Mystic Aquarium, horseback riding, golf, sailing, submarine tour cruises on river, Coast Guard Academy nearby. Excellent dining in area.

DIRECTIONS: take I-95 to exit 89 (Allyn St.); go north 1½ miles to light (Rte. 184 Gold Star Hwy.), Turn right and go east ⅓ mile. Inn is on left, up the hill.

The Jenny Lind Room.

BISHOP'S GATE INN

Theater people

Bishop's Gate Inn, located in the center of town, is a gem. Established by Julie Bishop, who worked with the Goodspeed actors, the theatrical tradition is being carried on by current innkeepers Molly and Dan Swartz.

Besides the full breakfast, which might include stuffed French toast, buttermilk pancakes, or hearty egg dishes, the innkeepers offer guests dinner if they request it in advance.

Each bedroom is completely comfortable and most display handsome early American furnishings and accessories. The Director's Suite is dramatic with its beamed cathedral ceiling, private balcony, and "Hollywood" bathroom complete with double sinks, sauna, and sitting area.

BISHOP'S GATE INN. Goodspeed Landing, East Haddam, CT 06423; (860) 873-1677; Dan and Molly Swartz, hosts. Colonial built in 1818 and filled with family antiques. Six guest rooms, all with private baths. Open year-round: $75 to $100 double. No children under six, no pets; Visa/MasterCard/Discover, checks accepted. Hearty full breakfast. Many wonderful restaurants a short drive away. Goodspeed Opera House, museums, state parks, Connecticut River cruises, airstrip on riverbank.

DIRECTIONS: from New York City, Providence, or Boston, take Connecticut Tnpke. (I-95) to exit 69 to Rte. 9. From Rte. 9, take exit 7 to East Haddam. Cross bridge and go straight on Rte. 82 for 1 block. Inn driveway is on left.

THE PALMER INN

Mansion by-the-sea

Skillfully crafted by his shipbuilders, this turn-of-the-century eighteen-room seaside mansion was constructed for Robert Palmer, Jr., an owner of the largest wooden shipbuilding company on the East Coast in its day. Today the house carries on as an elegant inn.

Tastefully furnished with Victorian furniture, period wallpapers, brass fixtures, and antique appointments, the inn boasts a good measure of family heirlooms. Original and unusual stained-glass windows add drama to the rooms, and lush flowers and herb gardens adorn the spacious grounds.

THE PALMER INN. 25 Church Street, Noank, CT 06340; (860) 572-9000; Patricia White, owner. Open year round. Six spacious guest rooms with private baths. Rates: $115 to $215; includes pleasant continental breakfast. Children sixteen and over; no pets; no smoking; Visa/MasterCard/American Express. Dachshunds on premises. Within walking distance of tennis, sailing, art galleries, swimming, and fine lobster house.

DIRECTIONS: take I-95 to exit 89, Allyn Street. From north take a right (and from south a left) and travel through two traffic lights across Rte. 1 onto West Mystic Avenue to stop sign. Turn right onto Noank Road (Route 215) and travel 1.7 miles to stop sign. Turn left onto Mosher, past fire house, and turn left onto Main Street. Go 1 block and left onto Church. Tall hedges surround inn. Guest parking in back of inn.

A seaside mansion crafted by shipwrights.

This public room, used for breakfast, is disarmingly colonial.

RIVERWIND INN

Collections everywhere

Riverwind, a delightful country inn, is nestled on Main Street in the Connecticut River Valley town of Deep River. Native Virginian Barbara Barlow has turned the rambling colonial-era home into a wonderful blend of New England charm and down-home Southern hospitality.

The décor is colonial, with an eclectic folksy touch. Featured are an extraordinary antique quilt collection, farm and cooking implements, dried herbs and flowers, hand-stencilled walls, and one-of-a-kind furniture, much of it from Barbara's family.

Eight guest rooms are charmingly appointed. The Havlow Room has an early pine bed with hand-painted rose panels on the headboard and an exquisitely embroidered "crazy" quilt. Zelda's Suite, a two-room Gatsby-era hideaway, and the Champagne and Roses Room are particularly romantic.

Barbara and her husband, Bob Bucknall, like to describe their place as "anti-formal." With eight common areas throughout the inn, guests can either mingle or find a special place to be alone.

There are collections of collections everywhere, from old playbills to handmade dolls. Pigs play prominently in the décor, owing to Barbara's childhood in Smithfield ham country. And the country breakfast usually includes pig-shaped biscuits.

RIVERWIND INN. 209 Main Street, Deep River, CT 06417; (203) 526-2014; Barbara Barlow and Bob Bucknall, owners. Open all year. Eight guest rooms with private baths and air conditioning. Rates: $90 to $155 per room, including full country breakfast. Children over 12 welcome; no pets; smoking allowed in common rooms; Visa/MasterCard/American Express. Famous Goodspeed Opera House, Essex steam train, riverboat cruises nearby.
DIRECTIONS: inquire when making reservations.

Innkeepers Bob Bucknall and Barbara Barlow.

INN AT CHAPEL WEST

New Haven extravaganza

Originally slated to become posh new office space, this eighteenth-century mansion has blossomed into a bed and breakfast on the revitalized upper Chapel Street. Once an unofficial Yale fraternity house, it is a fresh bouquet to the neighborhood and a symbol of New Haven's commitment to the restoration and reclamation of its heritage.

Eclectic in its décor, the guest rooms have faux marble door panels hinting at color schemes within. Room 34 has a cloudscape painted by Connecticut muralist Peter Perry, a brass bedstead, a pine hope chest, and soft lavender, pink, and blue appointments. Room 21 has a lace-draped day bed and Austrian shades, while Room 11 has Laura Ashley fabrics, a pressed tin ceiling, a velvet paisley chair, and Victorian face masks. All of the beds, piled high with cushions and goose-down pillows, are bedecked with ruffles and look wonderfully inviting. Some of the rooms have gas-lit fireplaces, and all of them have comfortable chairs, writing desks, telephones, and televisions. Bathrooms have pedestal sinks, blow dryers, and shower radios.

Continental breakfast, buffet-style, is served in the dining room and a catered dinner can be arranged. A tour of Yale, theater tickets to one of New Haven's many musical or dramatic offerings, transportation, and secretarial or baby-sitting services are happily attended to. The India Palace, Miya's, and Saigon City, serving Indian, Japanese, and Vietnamese food respectively, are literally a stone's throw away.

In addition to housing visitors to Yale and people on business, the inn has already had its share of celebrities. Chuck Norris slept here, as did the moms of Cybil Shepard and Sylvester Stallone.

THE INN AT CHAPEL WEST, 1201 Chapel Street, New Haven, CT 05611; (203) 789-1201, Fax (203) 776-7363; Melodie Pogne, innkeeper. Open all year. Ten guest rooms, all with private baths, telephone, color TV; some with fireplaces. Rates: $175 to $195, including continental breakfast. Children welcome; no pets; smoking permitted in public areas; all major credit cards. Handicap accessible. The inn is less than four blocks from Yale's Old Campus, New Haven Green, and minutes from New Haven's 30 plus pizza places.

DIRECTIONS: inn is located on Chapel Street, the main shopping street of downtown New Haven, leading to the green. Call for directions.

PHOTOGRAPH BY WILLIAM SEITZ

Room 33, with superb antique Victorian pieces.

JOHN KANE PHOTOGRAPHS

THE HOUSE ON THE HILL

Architectural gem

A legacy of Waterbury's heyday, when it was renowned for its brass and clockworks, this Stick-style Queen Anne Victorian was built by Wallace Camp, the inventor of the post office box. Along with other architectural gems, it remains to be admired long after Waterbury's era of wealthy mill-owners who erected them has vanished.

Built over a hundred years ago, the house on the hill has been lovingly restored by owner Marianne Vandenburgh. Original cherry, oak, and mahogany floors, fireplaces, and built-ins provide a backdrop that imbues the interior with richness and warmth. The deep rust walls in the parlor, with its velvet, paisley, and crewel work, combine with vintage

Left, top, the richly carved woodwork of the striking sitting room; bottom, an utterly charming guest room.

bound books, artfully assembled dried flowers, and lyrical sculpture to create the overwhelmingly romantic mood of *Victoria Magazine*.

The lace-filled breakfast room, with its down-pillowed wicker settees, is the setting for the corn-meal pancakes and homemade berry sauce that guests adore. Afternoon tea or sherry is served with homemade sweets.

The house affords the multi-talented Ms. Vandenburgh the opportunity to display her decorating, hosting, and culinary gifts. Even her acting ability has been tapped. When Jane Fonda rented the house during the filming of *Stanley & Iris*, Ms. Vandenburgh appeared in one of the scenes.

THE HOUSE ON THE HILL. 92 Woodlawn Terrace, Waterbury, CT 06710; (203) 757-9901; Marianne Vandenburgh, owner. Open all year. Five guest rooms, 4 with private baths, 1 sharing; all with English kettles. Rates: $75 to $125 per room, including full breakfast. Well-behaved children and pets welcome; no smoking; no credit cards; Spanish spoken. Concert series Feb-Mar.

DIRECTIONS: from I-84 to Waterbury take exit 21 and go right on Meadow St. (which becomes Willow) to Pine. Take right up hill past Woodlawn Terrace to first driveway on left, up to house.

WEST LANE INN

Sample the good life in a private mansion

A New England getaway close to city bustle, the West Lane Inn in historic Ridgefield, Connecticut, is just fifty miles from New York City. This bed and breakfast inn contains more rooms than most, so guests don't always share their morning muffin and coffee with owner Maureen Mayer. But they enjoy the solid comforts evident throughout this grand, early nineteenth-century mansion. Amenities generally found only in fine hotels maintain the prevailing sense of quiet and privacy. Bathrooms are equipped with heated towel racks, full-length mirrors, and, in some cases, bidets.

An adjoining house, called the Cottage, contains suites with service kitchens and private decks that open onto a vast expanse of well-manicured lawn. A simple room service menu, an optional full breakfast, king and queen-sized beds, a tennis court, and one-day laundry and dry cleaning service make the West Lane Inn a welcome haven for tired wayfarers and business travelers.

One mile away—a short walk past fabulous mansions—is the heart of Ridgefield village, with its public tennis courts, antiques shops, and an interesting selection of good restaurants.

WEST LANE INN. 22 West Lane, Ridgefield, CT 06877; (203) 438-7323; M. Mayer, innkeeper. Former private mansion invites guests to sample the good life. Open all year. Fourteen guest rooms in main house, two with working fireplaces; six suites in rear cottage, all with private baths. Rates: $100 single, $115 to $125 double, including continental breakfast; full breakfast available for extra charge. Good dining in area. Children welcome, cribs and play-pens available; no pets; major credit cards; no checks. Ridgefield offers Revolutionary War sites, tours, museums; cross-country and downhill skiing.

DIRECTIONS: from NYC, take the FDR to the Major Deegan to Saw Mill Pkwy. Stay on Saw Mill to end and exit onto Rte. 35 going east. Drive approximately 12 miles to Ridgefield. Inn is on Rte. 35.

A portrait of the son of the original owner hangs in the stairwell.

BUTTERNUT FARM

An impressive, small museum

Butternut Farm in Glastonbury, Connecticut, is an especially fine example of pre-Revolutionary architecture. The oldest section of the house was built by Jonathan Hale in 1720, a well-to-do gentleman with an eye for fine moldings and a feel for proportion—rare commodities in early homes. By the mid-1700s, a keeping room, "borning room," buttery, and extra bedchambers were added as Hale's family grew.

Present owner Don Reid is a faithful steward to this architectural gem. He loves early American antiques and has collected many excellent examples from the period, including an antique pencil post canopied bed, an exquisite cherry highboy, and pre-Revolutionary bottles and Bennington pottery marbles.

The keeping room has beams bedecked with drying herbs and flowers. An antique settle and variety of chairs surround the large hearth, whose magnitude is completely overshadowed by the second fireplace found in the adjoining dining room. This brick hearth, of mammoth proportions, is teamed up with an oversized antique dining table and bannister-back chairs. An oil painting of Jonathan Hale's son is prominently displayed.

Guest rooms upstairs are decorated with wing-back chairs, wooden chests, and antique hat-boxes. Museum quality, hand-hooked rugs brighten softly gleaming, wide-plank pine floorboards.

Continuously occupied since its construction, the house shares its charm with appreciative guests. A carefully tended museum of Americana, this inn is like another world—one that should be visited and revisited to enjoy its many facets.

BUTTERNUT FARM. 1654 Main St., Glastonbury, CT 06033; (860) 633-7197, Fax (860) 659-1758; Don Reid, host. Elegant house built in 1720, with a wealth of interesting architectural detail. Open year-round. Two guest rooms, shared baths; two apartments with private baths. Rates: $65 single, $65 to $83 double. Full breakfast. Checks and Visa/MasterCard/American Express accepted; no pets; smoking discouraged. Good dining in town and in adjoining Hartford.

DIRECTIONS: take I-84 or I-91 to Rte. 2 exit. Follow Rte. 2 and take exit 8; go right toward Glastonbury Center. Drive to Main St. and turn left. Drive 1.6 miles, and inn is on left. Enter from Whapley Road.

In the English country style.

MANOR HOUSE

One of Connecticut's finest

A beautiful turn-of-the-century mansion, the Manor House in Norfolk, Connecticut, with wood-paneled walls and huge fireplaces, is the setting for a bed and breakfast *par excellence.*

The eighteen-room house was built in 1898 by Charles Spofford, designer of the London Underground and the son of Ainsworth Spofford, head of the Library of Congress under President Lincoln. The interior is distinctly Victorian, with elegantly carved furniture, ornate fixtures, leaded-glass windows, and billowy curtains. Tiffany stained-glass windows and the cherry-wood paneling add warmth and luster to the interior.

Horse-drawn sleigh and carriage rides are pro-vided for guests, during the appropriate season, after breakfast of fresh farm eggs, bacon, orange waffles, blueberry pancakes, French toast, homemade breads, muffins, and coffee. The host, Hank Tremblay, a beekeeper, provides the honey with which guests top breads and various entrées.

The herb garden, replete with chives, oregano, basil, sage, and other exotic plants, lures guests in search of a clump to transplant in their own gardens.

Carl Dudash, a well-known local harpsichord maker, offers a free night's accommodation at the Manor House with the purchase of a harpsichord.

Yale summer chamber music concerts, an annual event, are within walking distance.

MANOR HOUSE. P.O. Box 447, Maple Avenue, Norfolk, CT 06058; (860) 542-5690 (same for Fax); Diane and Henry Tremblay, hosts. Open all year. Eight guest rooms, all with private baths, some with fireplaces and private balconies. Rates: $95 to $195 double; includes full breakfast. Children over 12 welcome; no pets (boarding kennels nearby). Yale Summer School of Music and Art an annual event in Norfolk; crafts, antiques, theater, golf, swimming, and skiing.

DIRECTIONS: take I-84 to exit for Rte. 8 north at Waterbury, Conn. Go north to end of Rte. 8 at Winsted and take Rte. 44 west to Norfolk and Maple Avenue. From Massachusetts take Turnpike west to Rte. 7 exit and go south to Canaan and east on Rte. 44 to Norfolk.

JOHN KANE PHOTOGRAPHS

An inviting country setting.

GREENWOODS GATE

Exquisitely inviting

Summer visitors to the Norfolk Chamber Music Festival may have discovered Greenwoods Gate. If not, they are in for a treat. This beautiful clapboard-and-shuttered colonial house bursts forth with equal chords of romantic ambience, exquisite furnishings, and sumptuous breakfasts.

George Schumaker, the new owner since 1993, has made his own mark on Greenwoods Gate by adding an impressive fourth suite that competes with the luxury of the other three. It is named the Lillian Rose Suite and has two bedrooms and a den with library and large bathroom.

The spacious Darious Phelps Room, in muted tones of peach and green, has upholstered peach headboards, matching comforters, and a perfume-laden Victorian dressing table. Adjoining is a bath with a six-foot clawfooted tub.

Separate from the rest of the house, the Levi Thompson Suite, on two levels, has rich native cherrywood and a luxurious spa with steam enclosure and whirlpool.

Covered in Ralph Lauren wall covering and fabrics, the E.J. Trescott Suite, in Delft blue and white, has a luxurious brass-and-iron bed, a handsome Empire chest, and a delightfully furnished four-story doll's house perched atop a blanket chest.

For breakfast, a buffet is set up in the center hall library as an eye opener to whet guests' appetite for the long, leisurely sit-down breakfast that is served by the fireside in the dining room. Entrées run the gamut from apple raspberry baked puff pancakes to feather bed eggs Español to baked eggs with Nova Scotia smoked salmon.

GREENWOODS GATE. 105 Greenwood Road East, Norfolk, CT 06058; (860) 542-5439; George E. Schumaker, owner. Open all year except Christmas and Thanksgiving. Four luxury guest suites with private baths. Rates: $185 to $215 per room. Includes full gourmet breakfast, afternoon tea and pre-dinner refreshments. Children 12 and over welcome; no pets but kennel nearby; no smoking; Visa/ MasterCard/American Express. Yale School of Music summer concerts in Norfolk; Tanglewood nearby. Winter cross-country skiing, summer golf and tennis.

DIRECTIONS: on Rte. 44 east of Norfolk village green ½ mile. Call for more details.

Where sweet dreams are assured.

BED & BREAKFAST RESERVATION AGENCIES

Connecticut

BED AND BREAKFAST, LTD., P.O. Box 216, New Haven, CT 06513; (203) 469-3260; Jack Argenio. Write, sending SASE, or call between 5 and 9 P.M. weekdays and any time weekends. Period homes, estates, farms, *125 listings statewide.*

COVERED BRIDGE BED & BREAKFAST, P.O. Box 447A, Norfolk, CT 06058; (860) 542-5944; Diane Tremblay. *Northwest Connecticut, southern Berkshires, Hudson Valley, and Connecticut shoreline, Southern Vermont.*

NUTMEG BED AND BREAKFAST AGENCY, P.O. Box 1117, West Hartford, CT 06127; (800) 727-7592, (860) 236-6698, Fax (860) 232-7680; Michelle Souza. 9:30 A.M. to 5 P.M. Monday through Friday. Vacation homes, restored historic homes, relocation. *Connecticut.*

Maine

BED & BREAKFAST DOWN EAST LTD., 39 Cedar Street, Belfast, ME 04915; (207) 338-9764, Fax (207) 338-3799; Sally Godfrey. Private homes at lakeside, countryside, town, or coast. *Maine.*

BED & BREAKFAST OF MAINE, R.R. 26, 377 Gray Rd., Falmouth, ME 04105; (207) 797-5540; Fax (207) 797-7599; Donna Little. Weekdays 6 to 11 P.M.; weekends 10 A.M. to 10 P.M. *Coastal, islands and mountains in Maine.*

Massachusetts

BED AND BREAKFAST ASSOCIATES, Bay Colony, Ltd., P.O. Box 166, Babson Park Branch, Boston, MA 02157; (617) 449-5302; Arline Kardasis. *Eastern Massachusetts.*

A BED AND BREAKFAT ABOVE THE REST, Box 732, Boston, MA 02146; (800) 677-2262, (617) 277-2292; Colleen Hartford. 10 A.M. to 4 P.M. Victorian townhouses and Beacon Hill homes. *Boston/Brookline, Cambridge, Cape Cod, Nantucket, Plymouth, Gloucester.*

BED AND BREAKFAST CAMBRIDGE AND GREATER BOSTON, P.O. Box 665, Cambridge, MA 02140; (617) 576-1492; Pamela Carruthers. 9 A.M to 6 P.M. Monday to Friday; 10 A.M. to 3 P.M. Saturday. Private and vacation homes of every description. *Boston, Cambridge, and Lexington.*

BED AND BREAKFAST CAPE COD, Box 341, West Hyannisport, MA 02672; (800) 686-5252, (508) 775-2772, Fax (508) 775-2884; Clark Diehl. Country inns, sea captains' houses, host homes. *Cape Cod, Martha's Vineyard, Nantucket, Gloucester, and Cape Ann.*

BERKSHIRE BED AND BREAKFAST HOMES, P.O. Box 211, Williamsburg, MA 01096; (413) 268-7244, Fax (413) 268-7243; Eleanor Hebert. *Private homes in western Mass. from Sturbridge to the Berkshires; southern Vermont, eastern New York state, District of Columbia.*

HOST HOMES OF BOSTON, P.O. Box 117, Waban Branch, Boston, MA 02168; (617) 244-1308; Marcia Whittington. 9 A.M. to 12 noon, 1:30 to 4:30 P.M *Covers Boston and select city suburbs.*

PINEAPPLE HOSPITALITY, INC., P.O. Box F821, New Bedford, MA 02742; (508) 990-1696; Robert Mooz. 9 A.M. to 5 P.M. weekdays. Homes or small inns. *Six-state area of New England.*

New Hampshire

NEW HAMPSHIRE BED & BREAKFAST, P.O. Box 146, Main Street, Ashfield, MA 01330; (413) 628-4033; Ernie Taddei. Country classics, waterfront, mountain views, farms. *New Hampshire.*

Rhode Island

BED AND BREAKFAST REGISTRY AT NEWPORT. 23 Catherine Street, Newport, RI 02840; (401) 846-0362; Ted and C.G. Critz. Restored colonials. Victorian mini-mansions, and homes by the sea. *Newport.*

HISTORIC NEWPORT INN ASSOCIATION, P.O. Box 981, Newport, RI 02840; (401) 846-7666. *12 Newport inns.*